**ANCHOR BOOKS**

EVERY KIND OF LOVE

Edited by

Sarah Marshall

First published in Great Britain in 2005 by
ANCHOR BOOKS
Remus House,
Coltsfoot Drive,
Peterborough, PE2 9JX
Telephone (01733) 898102

SB ISBN 1 84418 393 9

FOREWORD

Anchor Books is a small press, established in 1992, with the aim of promoting readable poetry to as wide an audience as possible.

We hope to establish an outlet for writers of poetry who may have struggled to see their work in print.

The poems presented here have been selected from many entries, and as always editing proved to be a difficult task.

I trust this selection will delight and please the authors and all those who enjoy reading poetry.

Sarah Marshall
Editor

CONTENTS

DREAMING OF MY LOVE

When I am dreaming and passing over thee
Open your arms and reach for me

Dreaming of your beauty
Laying in the dark

Your love pacing through the night
As if a giant spark

Your body gently resting
Peaceful and serene

How I yearn for you
And curse that this is just a dream

If dreaming is all I have of you
Then never shall I awake

Dreaming of you my love
My love I will forsake

Lisa Miller

THIS SPECIAL MAN

This special man keeps us warm
All through the day.
This special man, I love him
In each and every way.
This special man will never leave me
I love him in my heart.
If this special man leaves me
My life will tear apart.
So stuff this poem and celebrate
That this special man's my dad.
It's Father's Day for God's sake,
Let's all just go mad!

Chelsea Ballantyne (12)

TRAIN OF THOUGHTS

Gazing out the window of the speeding train
The scenery passing me again and again
My thoughts were upon you and all we had been
For they were the moments I'd shared with you
Just like a picture the landscape is there
With trees all around standing so bare
Rows upon hedgerow spoiling the view
But not my thoughts I have of you
Acres of fields with rivers in-between
Passing me by in shades of green
The only sound is the sound of the train
As it picks up speed once again
People around me are unaware
Of why I sit and lovingly stare
So I softly smile and silently say
It's because of the man I love today
That I have shared my thoughts of him
With the beautiful view I have within.

S Hamlyn

COREY AND JASMINE

Corey and Jasmine, you might never know
The love that is felt for you, wherever you go.
Circumstance says that you are apart,
But wherever you are, you are both in my heart.
A grandmother's love will always be near,
Wherever you are, you have nothing to fear.
When you grow up and may wish to know
From where you came and where you will go,
I hope you get answers which are very true,
That your father and family will always love you.

J Hagen

LOVE HURTS

My wife Doris' face at the window,
Watching me mow the lawn,
She smiles though I know she has some pain,
Her face is a little bit drawn.

When the mowing I've finished,
She still smiles with a nod
And says, 'That's lovely Charlie,
You've done a good job.'

My Doris is dying with cancer,
She knows she has not long to live,
And would never dream of causing a fuss
When there is so much more love she can give.

As long as I live, I shall always be glad
To treasure the memories of the wife I have had.
I loved her with every beat of my heart
From the moment we met, right from the start.

D eep in thoughts of my Doris
            and the wonderful life we've had,
O ne smile follows another,
            though tears fall, 'I'm not really sad.'
R oses deepen colour with sunshine,
            time deepens love, 'My heart knows.'
I really do wish my Doris was here
            so that once again I could 'Propose.'
S he will be smiling in my thoughts.

Charlie Peachey

I'M BLIND, SO WHAT!

I cannot see the skies above,
I cannot see the fluffy clouds,
I cannot see the birds,
I cannot see the flowers.

I cannot see my mum or dad,
I cannot see my brother,

But,

I can feel their touch,
I can hear their laughter,
I can feel their love in my heart.

You don't have to be able to see, to see that.

Devon Stewart (12)

SWEETS FOR MY DAD

We all like sweets.
You like sweets,
I like sweets,
Which sweets do you like the best?

We all like sugar sweets.
You like chocolate,
I like lollipops.
Which sweets do you like the best?

We all have tummy ache.
You have fillings,
I have no teeth.
Which sweets do you like the best?

Karen Salter (6)

LOVE LOST AT SEA

She goes down to the beach
Just as each day at six
Sometimes lights a fire
From driftwood and sticks

Then off for a swim
No matter how cold
To cleanse her of sin
And secrets so old

She thinks of the past
Times full of such joy
Before mould was cast
And she was quite coy

She dwells on the love
That's lost and is gone
Gone from this cove
And left her alone

They just could not be
Together as wished
He was married, not free
So in secret they kissed

When they were found out
She was cast from the town
He moved and shipped out
But his ship, it went down

So long gone, but still he is near
The ghost in her heart, the memories so clear
She's remained his and forever will be
For her man she sheds tears . . .

For her love lost at sea

Daniel Moore

SOULMATES

Do not weep for me anymore for I want to tell you I am here
I have been right beside you every day and drying every tear
Since I have left I've been with you, I never went far away
You thought I had as you can't see me or include me in your day
I know that you can't touch me or hold me so very tight
But I do watch over you during the day and while you sleep at night
I see you as you work, I see you kiss my picture before you sleep
You see I notice everything and also when you weep
So dry your eyes my darling and weep for me no more
For you haven't really lost me, I'm the other side of the door
Every door that you open, that's where I will always be
Giving you that cuddle that you often gave to me
When your work on Earth is finished and it's time to join me here
I will take your hand and lead you, you'll never experience fear
For then we'll be together and united again once more
Nothing can come between us for soulmates we always were

Margaret Ward

MY FRONT LINE MEMORIES

Living in London in the midst of the Blitz
Father would go out into the dark night
To do whatever was right.

The bombs kept dropping
People were dying
Buildings were turned to rubble
But still he helped his mates when they were in trouble.

Mummy would cry until his return
This was how about love I would learn.

I knew my daddy was brave and true.
He was one of the unsung heroes during WWII.

Elaine Priscilla Kilshaw

FOR GRANNY

You made his life hell for sixty years,
He should tell you some home truths, reduce you to tears
In your younger days you slept around,
Yet you demand respect and still seem proud
Of manipulating anyone you ever met
You haven't said a kind word yet
You cheated on your first husband, the doctor
The hand fate dealt you next really was a shocker,
Illegitimacy in the 40's was really frowned on
Divorce and remarriage was your only option
Free to marry poor old Grandad,
To control what life he previously had had
You used him and took him for every penny,
And kicked him out when he hadn't any.
You dumped your only child many miles away
Went back to the single life and have no remorse today,
Over the years you've got more selfish and stubborn,
Cruel remarks always hurting someone.
With your sharp tongue turning relatives away
Making friends with the mission you've started to pay.
You changed your last will for their company,
The homecare come in to make your tea,
To feed you your pills and tuck you in bed,
They don't really listen to a word you've said.
You'll be unhappy and bitter for the rest of your days,
It could have been different in so many ways,
You could have been open and loving and giving,
Then you would have a purpose in living.
So nearly departed, I'll have to forgive,
For me to move on, I've got my own life to live.

Claire Vittoria Lacey

LOVE...

He cradles me within his arms to keep the bad at bay,
Buried within his masculine chest wishing the world away,
He softly kisses my crown to soothe a troubled mind,
Bravely facing all clutter and sadness that he might find.

He intently listens to my strangest thoughts and dreams,
Slowly unlacing the ribbons that so tightly bind my seams,
He sees the beauty and loves the person I hold deep inside,
Not just fair of face but interested in the dark secrets I hide.

I laugh all the time with an unmistakable smile decorating my face,
My eyes possess a deep sparkle and my walk bears a gliding grace,
The sun seems to be eternally shining and the clouds are long gone,
The woes of the world wash off me and my happiness lives on.

The warm feeling inside from the morning rose left by bed,
Comforted throughout by all the kind words that are said,
Feeling so special like an angel lighting up someone's life,
And that he has been sent to protect me from worry and strife.

I see the eyes of a soul in the reflection of his eye,
Addiction increases, I need that constant high,
Of my heart he is the artery and of my body he is the limb,
Realisation dawns that I could not breathe without him.

Rhiannon Jones

MY DAD

He's funny like a bumblebee, flying in the air.
He is also cuddly, like a big, soft bear.
He always smiles like a happy little bunny
And I think he is really, really funny.
He's kind and gentle like a golden retriever.
My nan says he's handsome, but who would believe her?

Bobbie Heeks (8)

THE LONELY WEDDING DAY GUEST

So sad to be alone in a world full of hope
In my thoughts, no matter what, as distance is no fear
But still I wish you were here.

A few chosen days in a lifetime of living
What harm can that do?
Life, after all, is about giving.

The silence is worrying, but kept in my head
Outreached arms while sleeping alone in a double bed.

Today (the wedding day) an occasion of beginning
A very happy day for two people in love
Let's hope it stays that way with help from above.

I sit at the breakfast table and look across to an empty space
But wanted it really to be filled with your lovely face.
The bumpy road of friendship, of love and relationships is tough
Just wondering now if you have had enough.

Time for reflection, but maybe you have no time, always busy, busy
But still in this heart of mine you sit
But where in your life do I fit?

June Slater

DADDY

Dad you are the best,
Always there for me.
Driving a tractor,
Doing all your jobs,
You're the *best* for me.

Steven Salter (8)

THE ONE

You say that words are not enough
But that's all I have to say
You think that time has passed us by
But I still live for every day

You feel that you cannot love
But your heart is beating strong
You know your soul is who you are
But you still think that you're wrong

You see the world through open eyes
But you think that it's not real
You tell them all your sad story
But say that isn't how you feel

You say that you can't follow through
On all the promises you have made
You think the love that we have shared
Was nothing more than a façade

You won't let anyone in
Yet you expect to be invited
But the world doesn't work that way
I know because I've tried it

You say that this is over
But I think we've just begun
I won't give up my dreams for us
Not now I know that you're the one

Linda McGrath

WONDER BOY
(For my darling brother Chris)

As I watch you marvel at the world
Such innocence at your feet.
Such a being, so soft, so pure
Gingerly meandering from left to right
In, out, out of sight, such a little man
Commanding the site.
Oh to watch you sleep my angel
What a gift, yet your love
Concerns no rift.
Clip-clop go your feet as you venture
To the garden.
To meet who, what, I cannot say
Nevertheless, go on your merry way.
Diamond of diamonds, more precious still.
Now watching you still eat till you've had
Your fill.
Sleep well my little wonder
Let your dreams keep you
For now
Yet jealous I remain.

D J Skerritt

PRESCILIA

Prescilia is good at maths
And since
She has to be in school
Because
She has got cool ideas . . .

Prescilia Nkani (7)

THE MOON AND STARS

As I look up at the soft
And black velvet night sky
One bright silver moon
And starlit night
Your beautiful angel's face, dear Gemma
I can see there
In those sparkling stars up high

For their sparkle reminds me of
Your beautiful, black ebony eyes
And the bright silver moon
Reminds me of
Your wide and bright angel's smile
And both the moon and stars together
Dear Gemma
Remind me of how beautiful
You really, really are

Because you, my dear sweet Gemma
Are my five year old daughter
One of two beautiful angels
In my lucky life
The other angel's name is Margret
And she's my tender loving wife

Donald Tye

From Generation To Generation

Today I heard my father sing,
a song, for peasant and for king.
I'd never heard him sing before,
not that song, nor any more.

He sang it to my grandson - nine,
who sat and heard, with smile benign,
an old, old man of ninety-three,
who sang of an *England*, always free.

In age perhaps, decades apart,
yet joined together with one heart,
that says this land will always be
here to keep her people free.

No matter what the sceptics say
about the price that we will pay,
if the union we don't greet,
with outstretched arms and running feet.

There will, 'Always be an England', true,
if *she* means the same to both these two,
who cross generations, I do perceive,
love their country, I believe.

Brian Muchmore

INNER THOUGHTS

How could you deny this love that's so real?
Look deep within you to see how you feel
For pain isn't an option, your heart you should trust
This is really the loving and have it we must

Sorrow and heartache should not be around
It has no place here so push it underground
For all that I need from you, see, hear and touch
My darling, my hurting is unbearable so much

Please try to see what you can't understand
This is a thing in your mind not your hand
So find it you must, as it's so hard to bear
I cannot watch you hurting because it isn't fair

Think on now sweetness, as you know you must try
Because I am here and I don't want to die
Look inside your soul and I'm sure you will see
That one day you'll wish that you'd done it, you'll see

S C Matthews

DEAR FRIEND

No matter what I do or say,
You're never mad - always happy and gay!
When I'm in need, you're there for me,
My eternal special friend you'll be.

You're a precious gem, a real treasure,
Your true value I cannot measure.

Realising the golden value of our friendship,
(Though it has taken me a while),
You're my rock, I appreciate all you do
And you cheer me up when you smile!

Pam Sahota

UNTITLED

My dad lets me stay up late
He always likes to go out with his mate
He likes to tell jokes and wears a fluffy coat
He has a bald head and tells me stories at bed
He let my mum cut the wedding cake and has a daughter called Kate
       And I love him

He is very sweet, likes to be neat and
He tries hard for a job and has a friend called Bob
He never makes me cry
And likes climbing rocks that are high
He likes fixing doors and never gets bored
He likes cooking and does not like shoving
He likes kissing my mum and he is never dumb
He likes watching television and has good vision
He likes grapes and never minds snakes
He has two sons and likes to have fun
       And his name is Paul.

Ady Endicott (9)

LUCY PERCIVAL

(Dedicated to my great-great niece)

Lucy makes me think of spring,
And all things that April brings,
Those multicoloured early flowers
That lift their heads to catch the showers.

The ballet here and singing there,
She never seems to have a care,
To Lucy life is so sublime,
But then of course she's only nine.

Ernest Clinton Jones

SHARING

A life is very dull if there's no one there to share . . .

A loving embrace when feeling insecure . . .
A warm welcome when you walk through the door . . .

A listening ear when you need to talk . . .
A hand to guide you on a summer's walk . . .

A shoulder waiting when you need to cry . . .
A tissue in hand to wipe your eye . . .

A piece of advice when you need a guide . . .
A loving shadow when you need to hide . . .

A flattering word when you're feeling glum . . .
A helpful suggestion when you're feeling dumb . . .

A loving thought inside your head . . .
A cosy snuggle when you go to bed . . .

You've brought all the above into my life . . .
To make it complete, I'd like you as my wife . . .

Joanne Patchett

GRANNY AND GRANDA

What you did for us, we can never repay
You came to the 'Home' and took us away
Three motherless children, what a task to take on
You brought us up to be honest and strong

Our house was full of laughter and love
And now you watch over us from Heaven above
And in times of sadness we feel your touch,
Granny and Granda, we loved you so much.

Cathie Booth

MY FATHER

He wasn't just my father,
He was my dearest friend.
We worked together, side by side,
The days would quickly end.
People liked to talk to him,
He'd always make them laugh,
Talking of the old days,
Days well in the past.
If I ever had problems,
He'd always talk them through,
He'd listen and then advise,
I'd then know what to do.
Football and his garden
Were the things he loved the best,
But he had always time for me,
Now sadly he's at rest.
I never will forget him
For I miss him more each day,
All the little things we did
Are memories that remain.

Joyce E Barrett

WINDOWS OF THE SOUL

While you're asleep
And deep in dreams,
Let the stars that shine
In your eyes,
Glow in your heart
And let them sparkle,
With love for me.

Jacqueline Ann Johnston

FATHER'S DAY

Words,
Little arrows shooting down the telephone
Sweet little arrows with barbed ends
No,
You cannot see him today
We are busy
We have to polish the petunias
And shave the goldfish
You cannot see him today
We are busy
Perhaps tomorrow
We will be free

Yes,
Perhaps tomorrow we will all be free.

Susan Wren

THINK OF ME

Just close your eyes and think of me,
Of sunny days that used to be,
I know sometimes the tears will fall,
When memories you do recall,
But, you must remember too,
All the good times we've been through,
Just because you cannot see me,
Close your eyes and think of me
For we will never be apart,
My love lives on within your heart,
Just close your eyes and think of me,
Then by your side I'll always be,
So smile, while you remember these,
Our sweet and happy memories.

Trish Elliott

NIBO

My best thing in life
Would be my pet dog,
She is a pet Staffy
I love her a lot.
Her name is Nibo
She follows me everywhere I go.
She's nosy and funny
And playful too,
I couldn't be without her
I wouldn't know what to do.
It's only ever been me and my dog
We've looked after each other
She's been there a lot.
In times of sadness
She's always been there for me,
That's the way it will always be.
She runs around the house like mad
Shaking her toys in her mouth, she plays,
When she's gone
It will be lonely days.

Mary Woolvin

UNTITLED

My eyes see you
When you're away
My ears hear
Your unspoken words
My soul feels you
Every minute of the day
My heart utters
Before my tongue says
'I love you.'

Haitham Hafez

CELEBRATION!

It's coming, it's coming, it is coming - spread the word
Tell them it is coming until the whole wide world has heard
It is coming very shortly, hopefully on time
Tell them that the coming will be something that is divine
For it we have been trying and now it is to come
Put it into music then broadcast it to everyone
Excite those who are listening and it wish to hear
We cannot stop its coming, there is no way we would interfere
It we are expecting and it will come we pray
There will be no forgetting what will happen on that day
Others are helping to bring it all about
Even dogs are yelping as about it we do shout
Pass on please the message, tell it far and wide
It will be a blessing and that we cannot hide
For now the earth is moving as the moment does arrive
It our fears are soothing, we are so happy it is alive
It is coming, it is coming, there's a warming of the cold
This moment is so stunning I cannot wait for it to hold
To clasp it very closely - to feel the beating of its heart
Of course we will be rejoicing and we will never, ever part
It was coming, it was moving, we'd been waiting through the night
Now it's crying, she is now soothing, it is a beautiful sight
Through the hours we've suffered - we will not suffer any more
All those fears now succoured and it we will adore
We will share its coming - until its final morn
It has come and it is stunning - our *little* child *is born!*

Jon El Wright

An Orphan's Prayer

The little girl rushes home, crushing the sturdy grass,
As she avoids the tall coconut trees growing nearby.
In her hands she carries the beautiful flowers she has picked,
For the woman on a threadbare mattress, fighting a losing battle.
She stifles a sob and moans, 'Oh God, what am I going to do?'
Though she's been doing this for a while, she cannot bear to see it end.
Every day, after school, she puts away her books
And silently goes by her mother's side, waiting for a sign.
'What will I do if Mommy dies and goes up to Heaven?
Will God let me join her there, so I won't be alone?' she asked.
Her questions remained unanswered and the heavenly skies closed.
She frantically prays for a sign that He hears her prayers.
When the bird appears at the window sill, and chirps and sings,
It is as if He's been sent to instil a little life in her desperate vigil.
The answer is not what she expected, but it's enough to lift her spirit.
God is not silent after all, she mused; perhaps she just can't hear.
As she gets up and walks out, the bird follows.
Its wing on her shoulder feels like a breath of fresh air.
She suddenly knows that she will be all right if her mother dies.
Out in the marketplace, in the dust of unpaved roads,
She often came across other children just like her,
Roaming between the stalls at the Iron Market.
They don't look too unhappy, although dressed in rags.
If she goes there, there will surely be something to spare.
And every day the little bird will bring her news of her mother,
Fervently praying that another soul moves in to give her shelter.

Gladys Bruno

DAD

His water polo hands would lift and twist and throw
A ball or us around the garden in nice weather.
When he was home he did Mum's bidding with tellings off
When we would, 'wait 'til your father gets home' by shivering
$$\text{in bedrooms.}$$

The fights would break our hearts and we cried together to mend them,
Both strong, both right, both desperate to love again.
And when life was dark he wasn't always there, but hiding in his room
Not knowing what to do with me and my new anger.

We grew up with hearts and spirits tender and full of failings
But strong and getting stronger, like our bodies and our words.
While he gets weaker on his legs, and stops the twisting and
$$\text{the throwing}$$
His water polo hands have almost turned to holding.

Fiona Spotswood

EXPECTANT GRANDMOTHER

E very second takes a minute, every minute takes an hour
L istening for the telephone, the restlessness is dour
L onging for the answer that will make my day complete
I just cannot contain myself in expectation's heat
O rdinary people going here and going there
T his day to me so special, that nothing can compare
T he time just trundles on and on, it's almost now midday

G uessing the outcome, no I couldn't, no way
E very sound gets louder, as I wait for that phone call
O h please don't be much longer, I'm climbing up the wall
R acing now to answer it, petrified and torn
G reat news at last I'm hearing
E lliott George has just been born!

Jackie Davies

JOYCE

Life took Joyce from me as a sister early on,
But she returned, then left again.
A dark-haired, swarthy sister
In her, Father and Mother.
As I grew older, her visits I looked forward to,
There was always a bond.
I remember the egg and bacon breakfasts,
The talk, the news till late at night
Everyone wasn't pleased to see her
It's the price you pay for success.
As time has passed with its trials and tribulations of life
I know that deep inside she is a kind and caring, loving sister.
I miss her when she is not there
But look forward to the time
When she is there again,
Not just a sister, but a good friend
Who understands me.
Few people do.

R A Morley

MOTHER

A mother has looks of love and support on her face,
She is a person who is impossible to replace.

You can confide and confess, despite feeling uncertainty and fear,
But you're comforted by her understanding when she lends a loving ear.

She cares from cradle to adulthood,
She's always there, always watching, devoted, attentive, pure and good.

We feel blessed and special to be with our mother,
Because we could never receive so much affection from any other.

Kevin Clark

Da'

With a voice of gentle coaxing
draws out the understanding
of his children's temptations.
Compassionate with comfort
against the segregation
of the world, wiping the tears
from an isolated me.

Moulding the minds of siblings
into more defined variations
of what they wish to become.
Unmoved by the tantrums and sulks
manoeuvred to make the heart weak.

For himself he remains void;
society is not for him to judge;
as long as there is enough
happiness to go round,
his eyes gleam; dark, piercing,
in a house filled with song.

A constant pace neither exhausting
nor slow; allocates time to assess
every situation; making the job
do the work, until the shift is done,
with the home in array, tackles
the problem fresh in the door.

He's the motivator when everything
must: Go! Go! Go! A smooth jiver;
light, well balanced when the jukebox
is on the groove;
as all hail the homework king.

Darren Kelly

IT'S YOU I LOVE

Have I now found
the one I love?
The one who hugs pure hope
around me?

Does the one I love
also feel the contentment
when we hold each other's hands?
A circuit we complete.

Now we cut our paper for a week
but will the tear be sealed,
at the end of our part,
or will it be unsturdy?

I hope that together we will be sewn
until pain does dissolve
that loved, unique stitch,
as it's you I love.

Amy Herbert (13)

ROGER

I look for him everywhere and he's not there
not in front of the fire or behind the chair
he's not in his basket or asleep in the hall
he just isn't anywhere now, at all
I don't hear his bark when I open the gate
and my foot never accidentally kicks at his plate
no tiny feet follow, no tail in the air
no chocolate on Friday with tail wagging there
I look at the places where sometimes he'd be
and his absence prompts an odd tear
I can't see his brown eyes or peculiar ears
he isn't anywhere but he's everywhere

John Gilbert Slade

A BOY'S OWN HERO

Dad is long gone now - nearly twenty years.
I still see his face with the deep lines etched
At the corners of his mouth from the beers
He'd consumed with smacking lips - beer I'd fetched
Home in a jug from the pub. Dad appears
The way he was before the day he retched,
Puked, and lay back in his reclining chair
The cushion crushing flat his steel-grey hair.

Dad never got up from that chair again.
His body shrivelled like an old apple
Left lying on the ground in sun and rain.
He died within a week. At the chapel,
Unknown mourners said, 'He's been spared the pain,
Thank God.' But we remained, left to grapple
With grief at the dimming of those bright eyes
Hearts heavy as we said our last goodbyes.

But life does go on, pain passes. I see
Dad in my mind's eye still - giving pleasure -
Sipping from his pint pot of sugared tea
Telling tales of finding buried treasure
On ghostly wrecks in the Sargasso Sea -
Battling giant squids for good measure -
A boy's own hero fearless, strong and proud
By all life's terrors, and in death, unbowed.

Alexander Blackie

DADS

He's 6ft 3 and he's built like a tree
But he's very kind to me.
He picks his nose
And his grubby little toes
But
He's wicked, he's banging
He's absolutely smashing
He makes up rhymes when it's our bedtime
I love him oh so much.

My dad has size 10 feet and
Drives Mum mad as he's not very neat
But
He's got a vegetable garden
He burps and doesn't say pardon
He's mad about skiing, fishing and bikes
And when he sees scary movies he shouts
_ And screams, 'Yikes!'
But I love him oh so much.

Daniel Phillips (11)

GRANDMA

Grandma is my grandma
And she will always be.
Having fun with everyone,
Walking by the sea.

But even though she's eighty,
She's not like that to me.

She's been so kind to everyone,
And she's been kind to me.
I'm glad she's in my family
And that she can stay that way for me.

David Sheasby

THE SWEETEST FLOWER

Pretty flowers placed around
a simple granite stone,
remind me of the sweetest
of flowers I have known.
But even in their beauty
they still cannot compare,
to the beauty of the one
that's lying buried there.

Though planted in the garden
this earthly flower I know,
will bloom again some morning
where pretty flowers grow.
And they'll never know again
the pain and agony,
of the loneliness that now
is living here in me.

A wide array of flowers
in all their loveliness,
bring me back the moments as
again I reminisce.
Precious moments of the past
around a granite stone,
reminders of the sweetest
of flowers I have known.

James A Osteen Jr

A POOR FATHER'S DREAM

My father into a dream of mine
Colouring in rainbow dreams
To an obvious picture
Looking with an inner vision
He switched off his eyes.
A bad omen obfuscates a remark
Scrubbed with pitch-black
On my talents and goal
Filled up my heart and home as an empty vessel
Rapid pain stirs up into a solid particle
As a wounded scar
On my tearful eyes, my courage
A vitality flag rate into a glow
My father's ambition is winking as a star
In a stealthy manner to achieve success
Startles me a steadfast decision, to win my destiny
From Heaven, my father's blessings adorning,
What enchantment I am unable to express
I won my first step with a topper rank
Even my father, is afar to share my happiness.
It's a great tribute to my dad of my success
As before holding a doctor's degree
With a love of ambrosia
I gave life to his dream
He is alive in my heart ever and ever.

Bollimuntha Venkata Ramana Rao

LOOKING BACK

Looking back at all those years, it's now I truly see,
Without you there would be no me!
You used to be like a stranger,
How was I to know that we would end up together?

I am not ashamed to admit you were right,
On so many occasions you were my only guiding light.
Looking back now, it's your support and encouragement that
                                    had got me here
How was I to know you would always be there?

You were the one, who wiped my tears,
Held my hand through worst fears.
Looking back now, you taught me the true meaning of family.
How was I to know this is how it would turn out to be?

I am sorry if I ever neglected you,
To say the least I love you
And for all those lessons you taught me,
I listened carefully and truly.
And I promise you'll see,
A real improvement in me.

Chorin Kawa (14)

WHITE FIST ON WALKING STICK

Curving river, in the storm, torrential
In the flashes we can see the ramblers walking strong and straight
Notably keen to get to home at the top of the hill
Yet the ramblers miss the byway, the short cut in the storm.
From the curving river to the mountain house,
However we can see, even in the storm, they will endure to home . . .

Michael Soper

THE HOMECOMING

I have returned to England from the land of the didgeridoo
The land of the kangaroo, and there are quite a few.
For forty years I have lived in the Aussie outback
Rearing sheep, shearing the wool off their back.

For the first ten years our home was a wooden shack
Every amenity, especially water, we did lack.
All my life my favourite colour was green,
In this part of the world it was rarely seen.

For my dear wife Edna life was a long chore
What kept her going was our son Tom whom we both did adore.
He was educated sixty miles away
He boarded at the schools, at weekends he came home to stay.

Then he won a university scholarship in biology
It meant he would go to England to continue his study.
There he achieved his degrees, a fellowship, and a loving wife
He became successful, had a family, enjoyed life.

We missed him as any parent would
He had his own life to make, we clearly understood.
A few months ago Edna suddenly became very sick
We quickly got her into hospital, but that didn't do the trick.

She passed away in a deep sleep with little or no pain
Losing my love, there was no reason to remain,
Alone in the outback, my neighbour, the desert plain
Then I heard the most welcome refrain.

Tom and family offered me a home with them and retire
I gladly accepted, to return to England was always my desire.
I am now 74, have family love, share a warm home
Till my days run out I shall not be alone.
My homecoming will only be truly complete
When Edna and I sit together again on our divine seat.

Terry Godwin

OLD EYES (MY FATHER)

Do you remember
A golden age that time was?
Running through the cornfields
Free, just like the reliable sun.

Can you recall
The way the azure rivers flowed?
Catching fresh fish to eat,
Then catching cold.

Tell me another story, Dad,
Of the way things once were
Tell me the best times you used to have
Being the character that you are.

Let's go down the river, Dad,
Teach me to fish and dream.
Let's visit your old friends in faraway places
And buy mint ice cream.

I wish I could go wherever you go, Dad,
Go back in your time,
A time of appreciation,
A day in your life.

Katty King

GRAN

I survey the expanse of grass and sky,
And think of the unselfish love she gave
Only now I cherish the years gone by
And with remorse look upon her grave.

She gave me wealth, not in material form,
But love and values no money could buy.
Was there for me from the day I was born
And chastised me with no more than a look and a sigh.

Why is it so hard to show emotions when one is young?
Was I so unfeeling, I knew not her pain?
She had so many virtues that remain unsung
It was I, not her, that had much to gain.

I think of her often with love and tenderness
And wish I had told her how I felt.
But I must be content that she is now at rest,
Free from the hardship that life had dealt.

You never heard the sound of my voice,
My laughter or my cries of pain.
In your silent, locked-up world you had no choice
But Gran you will, when we meet again.

Anne Jenkins

HOLIDAYS WITH GRAN AND GRANDAD

When we visit Gran and Grandad
Good times are had by all
We don't have to wash the dishes
We don't have to clear the hall
We don't worry about housework
Grandma flicks the dust about
Then it's - 'Come on girls, we're ready'
And we're up and dressed and out
We go to visit castles
Lovely houses, parks and zoos
We picnic by the river
Where we all enjoy the view
When we go out shopping
Grandad always finds a seat
Gives us all some money
Says - 'Have yourselves a treat'
We always go to this hotel
Where we have to dress up - posh!
Grandad says, 'Have what you like'
And there's lots of lovely nosh
We're going home tomorrow
So we're feeling rather sad
But we're coming back for Xmas
And bringing Mum and Dad
We'll have lots of lovely presents
All piled around the tree
Lots of scrumptious things to eat
That Grandma bakes for tea
Dad says we are spoiled a lot
Grandma says that's true
But he was spoiled by Grandma
When he was our age too

They will come with us when we go home
Our turn to make a fuss
Then we'll spoil Gran and Grandad
When they come to visit us.

Lydia Barnett

FRIENDS

Since many years have passed by
Since time has flown and I remember
All the faces that have been and mean so much
So clear to me, I care to touch
Young cheeks and smiles
Yet miles and miles
Are set between us now
And how I long to see
Mal, Lizzie, Jane again
Shirley gone, my father too
Marie Jose, you passed through
Jacquie, Gill and Enid, Crid
Lorraine, Lorraine, Lorraine
Sue too, then you, my Janet dear,
Cathy I see, Elaine, Angela,
Melanie, Lydia still here
And Ruth in truth
Some yes still contact close
This means the most
And eases loss of time
These friends that remain mine.

Susie Powell

MY GARON

He never, ever spoke,
He only looked at me and smiled,
Lifting my heart with his love
And filling my days with his joy.

Because my days were his
And his were mine,
We whispered secret thoughts
And private fears.

We shared our burdens
Tears and cold distress
And warmed ourselves
Each in the other's love.

And now he's gone.
A sudden thought can bring a tear,
A half-seen blur of black and white
Across the field is called
In vain . . .
He will not come again.

Patricia M Smith

LOVE YOU ALL

I love my mummy
And my daddy too
Oh and my little sister, Khiaya
And not forgetting
My little cousin Moo
I love my nanny dearly
And my uncle Jason too
Oops I nearly forgot
My aunty Nicky
Oh dear, that won't do.

Cheyanne S Houghton

A MOTHER'S LOVE

How wonderful is a mother's love,
So helpful, trusting and true.
But this you never realise,
'Til she is parted from you.
'Tis then you think of days gone by,
And wish that she were near,
To help you on life's treacherous paths,
With a smile and a word of cheer.
An outstretched hand to help you,
If you should stumble and fall.
In return she asks for nothing,
But would gladly give you all.
So to those who have a mother,
Cherish her with care,
For you know there'll be no other
To fill her vacant chair.

Agnes Driver

A SHORT NOTE TO SWEETIE

Dear Sweetie Caroline

In your house will I dine
with my friends, we will count to nine.
To buy, forget not my favourite Chinese wine.
I wish to drink it under my tall pine,
which came as a gift from the mine.
May this note find and leave you still fine
for my love is always in each line,
because I know forever you are mine.

Your Valentine . . .

Nyasha John Musimwa

DISCIPLINE

Your behaviour seems unbelievable.
I try to explain but you don't listen.
A second and third attempt,
all gentle coaxing until the inconceivable,
I snap.

'I shouldn't have to ask you twice,' I say
whilst silly noises or faces you pull.
'But I only wanted to . . .'
'Yes,' I interject, 'act your age!'
I yell.

But then, when you *are* older
and you've moved on your way
you'll ring me so infrequently,
chat mundanely, about this and that
until you're only in my heart; not by my side.

You won't want me nearby.
New friends and colleagues will fill your time.
Try not to remember me as the mummy that yelled,
just a bit of discipline,
I tried.

Anita Curnin

THIS IS YOUR LIFE

Friday the 13th was the day you were born
In August '54 at 2.30 in the morn.
Eight pounds twelve ounces is what you did weigh
Quite a bit different than we now see today.

A happy, contented little boy
You were loved by everyone,
Including our elderly neighbours
The Arnups and Nichols with whom you had lots of fun.

At school you always obtained good results
At maths you were one of the best,
Woodwork and technical drawing too
You were up there with the rest.

On leaving school at chartered accountancy you tried your hand
But the motor trade won the day,
Buying, selling, now delivering posh cars near and far
You're really good at finding the way.

Now you've made your way to the big Five 0
In the company of Debbie, your wife,
And Christopher and Daniel, your two lovely boys
So David at 50, 'This Is Your Life'.

M Weavers

MOTHER I LOVE YOU

If ever a flower should bloom so true
There'll never be anyone just like you
For you mean everything to me
Yes darling Mother, I love thee.

You showed your love to me each day
You showed me love in your own sweet way
You scolded, you shouted, when I did wrong
Mother, dear Mother, it did not last long.

A bunch of flowers tells you how I feel
To show you in my heart what you steal
To say it with chocolates to sweeten your way
Thank you for all those wonderful years.

Years roll on and what you taught me
I've passed to the grandchildren, can't you see?
This day is yours, no words can repay,
Now I'm a mother, but you're still my mum!

R Duncan
(The instant song man)

A LOVE SONG

What is the purpose of a love song?
Other than for one person - to enthrone.
Composed in compulsion and desire,
to transfix one mortal being - higher.
Starting from a single inner emotion,
transforming to consumption,
stronger than a magic potion.
Replaces simple words, as we contrive,
to embrace another
                    - to share our lives.

Gary J Finlay

YOU

Amazingly loving and friendly you are,
Brightly you shine like a luminous star.

Innocent and mature in all your ways,
Glamorous you'll remain all of your days.

Ambitious, considerate and loyal to me,
Influencing others to be like you be.

Laughter from you is inevitable,
Fragile you are, yet unbreakable.

I just wanna thank God for you.

Wonderfully special and gentle you are,
You seem so close to me, yet you are far.

I don't want to lose you in this life,
Even though I'll meet you in the heavenly skies.

Miriam Appiah

KNICKERS!

My grandma wears her knickers on her head
Fills the passer-by with dread
And with this strange display of underwear
Takes visiting salesmen unawares
'And why such a habit?' I hear you cry
(I hope they're clean ones, by the by)
To keep her hair clean so the muck don't show
(She's a secret exhibitionist you know)
'And why not wear a headscarf?' you reply
They're not as versatile as knickers, that's why!

Susannah Pickering

MY BEST FRIEND SUE

Here's a little story
about my best friend Sue.
When I moved down here
she was the first I knew!
She was always smiling
never saw her frown,
she never, ever let things
get her down!
Then one day it happened,
she came in looking sad,
'I've got something to tell you
something really bad!
We're off to a new life
I thought that you should know,
we're going to America
that's where they want to go.'
Well that really shocked me
such a big surprise!
Then I looked right at her
and saw there in her eyes
both fear and excitement
mingling with the pain
knowing that she'd probably
never see me again!
Well now that she's been there
for a year or two
we're still in contact
through e-mails - quite a few!
So I think we've proved that
no matter how far away
we are still as friendly
as we've been since that first day!

And so I want to tell her
I want to make her see
no matter where she's living
she's still 'my friend' to me!

Rowena

DAUGHTER

Golden daughter,
woven hair waves gently
kissing the breeze.
Shining!
Reflecting light, radiating love.
Rejoicing!
Doe eyes dancing,
soul smiling
with God's glow.

Gracious gift,
given to me,
yet never belonging to me.
With tiny body
and a heart that embraces the world.
You envelope my life.

Melting anger,
mending pain,
bestowing meaning
of unquestionable faith.

I am humbled.
Words cannot do you justice.
My daughter . . .

Tracey Levy

FOR MUM

There comes a time when every girl
Must leave her family home
As every bird must leave the nest
And learn to fly alone
There've been many times I've hurt you
But remember I've hurt too
I want to live the life I choose
But the hard part's leaving you
You've taught me everything I know
You've shown me right from wrong
You've made me into what I am
You've helped me get along
And now I'm all grown up at last
No more a little girl
It's time for me to go out there
And make it in this world
Don't worry Mum, I love you
And no matter where I go
I will always be your daughter
And I have to let you know
That although we've fought and argued
Over petty little things
It's just that I was growing up
And had to spread my wings
I love you more than ever now
That I'm old enough to see
Just how much you've sacrificed
And what you mean to me
It's time for me to say my thanks
For all the years of love
For even though I'm leaving home
You'll always be my mum

With love
Debbie xxx

Debbie

MUM'S SONG

All the love songs I ever wrote
I thought for other women
Were all for you
And when they missed the boat
I forgave them
As you would have me do
You're not much physically now
But you're beautiful just the same
Every woman I'll ever love
It will be in your name

The times I got my fingers burned
Was up and then came down
It was all for you
I hope I took what I learned
And wore it like a crown
As you would have me do
You're not very worldly
But you're clever just the same
You showed me how to love
And I will do it in your name

I've been sitting thinking here
And this song just seemed to flow
And it's all for you
It will always be there
Even though I might go
On to something new
And if life and love and God
Could be added up in one sum
It would add up to two little words
And those words are - my mum

Paul Monaghan

ANNIVERSARY MAGIC

We all need a little magic in our lives
The need for fun and laughter still survives
The daily grind of life
The times of stress and strife
We all need a little magic in our lives.

We all need a little love to light our day
Someone to show they care in every way
To boost us when we're down
To smooth the wrinkled frown
And help us find the sun when skies are grey.

Today there's love and magic in the air
On this special day I'll show you how I care
I give this verse to you
To show our love is true
And we'll spread our love and magic everywhere.

Mary Daulton

MY DAD

My dad is always there,
Even though he's got bad hair!
He comes to me when I shout,
It doesn't matter what it's about.
Dad supports me at whatever I choose,
I have no pressure to win or lose.
I have a brother, a sister too,
He's there for all of us, he doesn't choose.
All I need is to do my best,
My dad will help me with the rest.
I love my dad with all my heart
We will *never* be apart.

Bethan Owen (10)

MY SON

My son, he is a special lad, talented, kind and true,
Enthusiasm flows round his veins, it oozes through and through,
If anyone tries to quash this, you do not want to be around.
He has a sixth sense that cannot be drowned.

He seems to know just what to do in situations bound,
He always gets it right,
Although sometimes we go through some sort of plight.
Like me he suffers from depression,
Sometimes he takes things near to obsession.
That is just the way he is,
Focused, steadfast and true, always thinking of routes to get through.
Twisting and turning, breaking the boundaries,
Things must be done; he will never give up until his race is won.

Janey French

GRAN

Quiet and peaceful, she sits in her chair,
I'm sure she must wonder, do we notice her there?
Her vision is failing, her hearing is too,
But in spite of these things she knows who is who.

Just a word or two spoken will light up her smile,
As we get her attention she talks then a while;
It takes little effort to brighten her day,
A bit of affection can go a long way.

There's no need to hurry as time past it ticks,
For why should she rush now she's aged ninety-six?
She rests or she snoozes, it's years since she ran,
But her mind is still agile and we love her . .
Our gran!

A O McBride

MEMORIES OF MY FATHER

My father taught me all I know,
it seems a million years ago,
gentleness always at the fore,
lingering at the very core
of his paternal love for me,
given freely, oh that he
could be beside me still
instead of lying on the hill.
I know now what he meant to me
before his passing set him free
to gain at last his well earned rest,
deserved for love that stood the test.
The little things I left unsaid,
now remembered in my bed,
too late to tell the one who mattered,
so often now my dreams are shattered
by memories of his love unstinting
given without a touch of hinting
that it should be returned as well
to the one who would not tell
the badness of men, but only the good.
With God's help I hope I could
be just like him and fondly pin
my hopes upon my kith and kin.

Frank J Mills

CRYOGENIC

The winter snow soaks into my hands,
They become numb with cold,
Icing my blood, freezing it
Into blocks of red distress.
Twilight moves over my body,
My frozen tears waiting for the
Warm kiss of your living soul.
I wait, already dead from passion spent.
My eyes reflect the daylight,
The spent day when I was moving
Under your whispers, into my heart.
Now a frozen tomb is my place,
Now I have no care to be careless.
I stare at the moonlight now,
It falls onto my face but
Does not melt my tomb.
The sun will rise as usual in the east
Where the coldest wind
Blows over the mountains.
I lie in wait for my thoughts,
Oh, I labour not now.
The wind blows my body
And scatters my ashes in a rush
Of white fury beyond the horizon.

Glenda Stryker

MADE IN ENGLAND

(Dedicated to my parents G and S Mehmet)

Up at dawn, no time to yawn, for my mother this is the norm.
Her body is weary, her hands are worn, pin-pricked fingers all
battered and torn.
She makes ties for a living, from morning 'til night,
sews them all up and presses them right.
Off they go with the lady next door, beautiful silk ties for the rich
to adore.
The labels say 'Hartnell' but we know much more, created by 'G'
who's been up since four.
Sold in Harrods, to the high and mighty, hand-made silk ties at
inflated prices.
Threading needles is not very nice, when you are young and want to
get on with your life.
Endless cotton bits on the floor, cushions stabbed with needles
punctuated and sore.
Twenty-four-seven, 'G' toils and sweats, in a back room in
Bermondsey, she expects nothing less - only to work hard and do
her very best.
What did she expect when she came to this land, a young girl of
seventeen, with no language at hand?
For fifty-one years she has struggled along, sacrificing her dreams
in order that we never have to be in the same position as *she*.

My father works hard for his money, waiting tables is not
very funny.
'Til two in the morning, and then up again at six,
Four hours sleep on a bare kitchen floor, with only used tablecloths
to lay down as sheets.
Aching feet and tired legs, for a grateful tip, you have to be seen to beg!
The rich and famous, he's at their beck and call and only he knows
what goes on behind closed doors.
For fifty-seven years he has struggled along, sacrificing his dreams
in order that we never, ever have to be in the same position as *he*.

T Kemran-Mustafa

MY AUNT'S LETTER LESSONS

She taught me to pen a letter of request to true perfection
Where every letter shone with a rare elegance
On soft blue, creamy paper with a sweet fragrance
No writing with jerky hands or mouthing a pen

I had to place every word in a ritually defined place
Like a king putting figures on an old sacred chessboard.
Where every word would not trespass on another's space
I wrote with an exactitude that drove me half-insane

Just one error and it would be all over again
The impurity in one left mistake was as heinous as
Disfiguring an icon.
It was just not done!

A correctly written letter seemed like magic
Transfigured paper with a glamour that would shake off demons.
And I felt like a gentleman of letters
Writing words in mysterium.

Stephen Wilson

WHEN YOU HAVE LOVE

We'd been apart some fifty weeks on two sides of the Earth
Our jobs had separated us for all that that was worth
Of course we kept in touch each day as we felt so alone
The highlight of our waking hours was reaching for the phone
We lived in different time zones and the weeks rolled slowly by
Our only happiness was being under the same sky
But finally the time had come to re-unite as one
The clouds of misery and tears were banished by the sun
And when we saw each other, we just held each other tight
To be apart for oh so long, we knew it wasn't right.
But now we were together, lost in love and all its glory
When you have love like we have love, your life's one big love story.

David Whitney

THE POND

I was hidden in a mere pond
I was in the shallow end
Not knowing where I was swimming to
Tangled up in seaweed
I could not see my reflection
My pond needed to be cleansed
I had fish surrounding me
But I never felt free and content

You, like a diamond, had fallen into my pond
You made the water turn from brown to blue
Like a star you reflected on my pond
The dust you sprinkled made the water sparkle
When you touched the pond the water lilies would bloom
Your smile would grab the attention of the waves
Your eyes were as pure as the pearls of the sea
At the mere sight of you all the fish in the sea would salute you

I saw your hidden dignity
I saw your generosity and gentleness
You made me see people for what they were
You made me see things I couldn't see
You taught me that life is about believing in yourself
And that without dreams nothing could ever become true
You taught me to become strong within and have hope

You threw a rope into my pond
I felt free with your presence
And now you have left
Leaving me to swim the ocean on my own
You sacrificed your love for my happiness
A love I thought I would never feel
My teardrops would never reflect the respect I have for you
I hope that one day you will find your own ocean.

Jasmine Choudhury

My Beautiful Child

From a twinkle in your father's eye
To the birth of a newborn cry
You sleep, we listen out for breath
You held it so long, scared us to death

Transfixed with every move you make
Excitement with a smile, the wind you break
Dress you up and show you off
Worrying times when you cry or cough

Cooing and smiling is perfect joy
Sitting, crawling with your favourite toy
Your first wobbly steps and terrible twos
First little word, first pair of shoes

Toddling around, needed eyes on my bum
First day at nursery, crying for Mum
No more nappies, dummies in the bin
Big school in September, your journeys begin

Watching you grow and learning the ways
Growing so fast from baby days
Teaching you the dangers of drugs and pills
Now you teach me in computer skills

Plodding along trying to keep hold of your reins
Time to cut slack for mistakes and gains
Relationships and fall-outs for you to explore
For experience of life I can teach no more

Go my beautiful child, it's time to spread your wings
As my tear trickles, for whatever life brings
Such an empty feeling without you at home
You can always come back if you ever feel alone

R S Wayne Hughes

THE GIFT OF LIFE

Who nurtures you for the whole of your life?
Who takes all the brunt of your trouble and strife?
Who loves and protects you, yet would never moan?
Who's there when you're in urgent need of a loan?
Who gives you the benefit of knowledge you'll need?
Who gives you advice you should always heed?
Who teaches you manners and how to behave?
Who teaches you how to spend money and save?
Who, when you're rude and offhand, loves you still?
Who stays up all night with you when you are ill?
Who cries when you leave home, mature and grown?
Who's still always there on the end of the phone?
Who do you love dearly, respect and admire?
Who sets you examples to which you aspire?
You owe the gift of life to your mother.
Treat her like gold, for you'll not get another.

Julie Wealleans

TO OUR GRANDDAUGHTER TANYA

A lovely girl is she,
Serving with the Royal Artillery,
She is over in Iraq.
We can't wait till she comes back.

Letters and parcels to and fro,
It's always like this when they go.
You worry and wonder how safe they'll be,
They are there for six months before they are free.

Then home they will come, let's hope safely.
We miss our Tanya as do all relations
Of our soldiers by their stations.
God bless our soldiers and bring them home safely.

Zoe French

DAD

When I think of you, I think of the wind in my hair
The yellow on the daffodil, the apple and the pear
Everything that's natural, not tainted by life's hardships
Everlasting gobstoppers, funny sounding friendships

Bacon sizzling on the shovel, graveyards quiet and dark
White steam, whistling, walking through Stanley Park
Funny stories about the war; the dog you wanted to keep
And how you crashed your steerie cart
On the hill that was too steep

Mostly I remember our walks and the ground we covered
The plants, the trees and the flowers, the priory we discovered
You'll always be in my heart which means I'll never be sad
You taught me everything I know because you are my dad

Sandra Roberts

SINCERE THOUGHTS

When I was young my parents were strict
I was always bad and so I was hit
But this has become a thing of the past
It taught me how to grow up fast
They taught me the powers of right and wrong
And this has made me very strong
I love my parents with all my heart
I dread the day we will be apart
I sometimes weep at the thought of them dying
I can't live without them, if I could, I'd be lying
If I had my time to come again
My parents would remain the same
I would never change the way they are
I love them too much by far and far

Susan Brown

GRANDPARENTS

Smiles on my grandchildren's faces
looking into their angelic little eyes
Time passes by with the ticking of the clock,
before you realise one summer's day long, long ago,
filled with happiness and joy
Watching my son playing with his grandad
when he was a boy

Having a holiday break in the
country at a favourite haunt of mine
Days of bliss and solitude relaxing
counting the clouds one at a time
Our chosen spot was a river running
fast opening up and getting wider
My son off exploring had returned
with a big, black, hairy spider

Seeing his grandad lying with his face
on his arms on the ground
Went over to disturb his peaceful sleep
and show him what he had found
Trying to arouse the old man
his enthusiasm he seemed to lack
Decided to let the big, black spider
crawl up his grandad's back

Life isn't full of honey trying to
enjoy the well-earned rest
Wrestling to shake off a spider put
on your back by the little pest
His body nearly turning somersaults
trying to shake the spider off
Exertion had been too much for him
as it made him loudly cough

His little darling angel had turned
into a devil in disguise
The pranks he was getting up to
before his very eyes
Walking back across the fields
to enjoy a rich, rewarding tea
The boy's face so full of innocence
being as good as he could be.

Raymond Thomas Edwards

TO MY MOTHER

Mother, you have done so well,
You deserve to hear that.
A life filled with courage you have led,
A foundation for so many.
Your determination, a precedent,
Your love and hope, a gift to all.
The child you raised, a woman now,
With a child of her own,
Realising how brave and strong you are.
It is now I understand all you have taught me,
It is now I realise your worth.
My greatest friend,
You have never failed,
Always a constant in my changing life.
In the playground and in the battlefield,
You are my rock,
My mother,
My loving other.
You have done so well,
And you deserve to hear that.

Dee Radia

MY FRIEND PAM

Eighty
Not weighty,
Flirty
Thinks thirty.

She's reckless,
She's charming,
Completely
Disarming.

Forgiving
Rewarding,
Talks without end.
I know it,
I love it,
She's my best friend.

M Andrews

SORE PAW

Dad hurt his finger,
The pain did linger.
He moaned and he groaned,
He said it was throbbing,
And did a bit of sobbing,
He went a bit pale and white,
Gave Mum and me a fright,
He stuck his head between his knees,
While Ivy made a cup of tea.
Mum wrapped it,
And strapped it,
Then stuck it in a sling.
'It still hurts,' he moaned,
Then carried on digging!

Ivy Horner (10)

AVIA

(A Litany for Grandma)

Steely-eyed Regina
Lady of the grey locks
Dove of domesticity
Blesser of birth
Donor of being
Dealer of doubt
Teller of tales
Sober governess
Doyen of doing
Mistress of giving
Broker of pain
Bridger of death
Portal of laughter
Gate of affection

Quaint priestess
Spangled prophetess
Vestal virago
Sorceress of drudgery
Harlot of husbandry
Slut of complacency
Madam of madness

Substance of woman
Woman of substance
Prowess of truth
Largesse of life . . .

Madonna mine.

Gol McAdam

OLD MAN'S BEARD OR TRAVELLER'S JOY
(Clematis Vitalbis)

One autumn,
Speeding
To a distant town,
Down a road lined with trees
Veiled in thistledown,
Dad suddenly said,
'How I laughed as a child
At the funny name -
'Old Man's Beard' -
For such a pretty plant.
I little thought I'd one day be
An old man with a white beard.

Though now I'm an old man
And my beard is white
It is still a joy
To travel the road
Lined with trees
Veiled in thistledown
With you children laughing
At *my* funny white beard.'

Speeding down the roads,
Lined with trees
Veiled in thistledown
I remember with joy,
My dear dad
With his lovely white beard.

Georgina Treeves

DAD

Hi Dad,
You alright?
I was thinking the other day
D'you remember my first trip to the pub with you?
New room, Sunday lunch, September 1965
14 new candles on my birthday cake

'Don't turn round
The man behind you is a bobby,'
My half of bitter went flat.
Friday night, five years later
Last pint in the club with you,
Always a good one

Sunday lunch
Newky Brown special
Followed by Mum's lunch.
Stag night you were there
My mates liked you
A good bloke, stood your corner

Wedding day,
Solid.

Your first grandchild saw you quietly elated.
Second grandchild saw you quietly elated.
Now I know how you felt.

You didn't see the new house, did you?
Pity, you would have liked it.

You're a good listener,
Don't say much,
But then, you died twenty years ago
I still miss you

Alan McKean

WHEN YOU'RE THERE MOTHER

Whenever I see you, Mother,
I feel so protected.
When you stroke me gently
You know I'm resurrected!

Now that I'm away from you, Mother,
I love you even more.
Treasure all memories in my heart,
And remember days of yore.

When your blessings are with me, Mother,
I'm away from suffering and pain.
When you hold my hands, Mother,
Among all odds, I can sustain.

Shanu Goyal

IF GRANDAD WAS ALIVE

If Grandad was alive in my time
I could have met him in Manchester
and laughed and joked about the factory
where I worked.
And spent hot sunny days with him
admiring the flowers.
And in winter we could have sat by the fire
and I'd have read him some of my writing
and watched the snowflakes outside.
And maybe we could have gone to Blackpool together.
Grandma could have come too.
If only Grandad had been alive when I was born
there was a lot of things we could've done.

Rachel Van Den Bergen

COLD AND DARK

The day is cold and dark
That is how I feel
Illness chills my body
Exhaustion darkens my mood

I want to be looked after
To be pampered and pandered to
To have my every mood anticipated
So I can do nothing

For that's all I feel capable of today
Nothing
Not cooking my meals or organising my day
I want to do nothing

I want someone to make my decisions
Someone to take on all my responsibilities
Because today
My body and mind want to do nothing
And I agree with them

Sarah Auld

AFTER HER TOUCH

And her sweetness still lies
like patient honey upon my lips
her silent gaze, bright
- the needle shine of stars - illuminating
my darkest shadow that wild,
secret place no one before her
has ever dared to touch.
Safe in the folds of her caress
the courage of my heart
becomes greater than the pain
of sad lovers, forlorn.

Neil Rogers

MOTHER TO MANY, THOU A MOTHER TO ME

How I wish to write like those poets prime
We peruse their works sublime,
But the more I muse on the words to pen
To make this poem transcendent feign,
The more my sight declines
To mere shards of dusty rhymes.
Let me therefore write truly,
I desire no more musing aid
And believe me that I said,
Mother to many, thou a mother to me.

I penned thy beauty
But thy beauty, it's poetry,
I then penned thy care of love,
Which is as dear as a dove,
For He liking himself so,
He that made thee whole,
But thy care is all bearing,
And never to be repaid
Therefore believe me that I said,
Mother to many, thou a mother to me.

Oritsegbemi Emmanuel Jakpa

MISS YOU DAYS

The days are shorter and the mist lies late;
The hedges blaze with berries and the leaves
Die in a shower of red-gold fire.
And I remember you and days of joy
When we kicked the leaves and laughed
And ran; our cheeks grew roses;
Now mine grow tears;
Do you feel this way
At this time of year?

Betty Norton

My Never-Sung Song

If I could sing you an ode, I would
But would you listen?
It's a song from my heart
My never-sung song

If my heart tore apart,
Would you mend it?
Would you care?
If my tears ever dropped on your palms,
Would you feel them?
Would you cry with me?

People say life is a farce
I say it could be worse without the one
You care about
Feels like I have been dipped in a mire
But who would pull me out?
I have sat gazing into the sun day long, thinking
Maybe you would listen to my song,
Maybe you would sing with me
Maybe you would dance with me

I will wait, I will keep singing what looks like
My last song
Waiting for my last dance with you
Hoping to see the smile on your face
This is my never-sung song
I sang it for you
But danced to it all alone

Joseph Iregbu

FOR MY SISTER

(To Karen from Linda - September 2004)

The letter in her hand confirms her worst fears
Nothing now can stop the tears
Until that moment, the chance had been slight
But the words are stark; the glimmer now out of sight

The stick in my hand leaves me in no doubt
Two pink lines have appeared, do I sit down or shout?
From here on in, things will never be the same
So I need her to know, I feel her pain

Mother Nature seems cruel and life so unfair
One sister feels delight; the other, depths of despair
How can this be - the main question is why?
Maybe answers we'll find as time goes by

We've always been close and great times we've shared
If only this heartache we could have been spared
What the future holds now, we cannot see
But dear sister she is, and best auntie ever she'll be

Linda Purves

DANGEROUS LOVE

I would play that dangerous game
If you would only do the same
Just to spend one night with you
Is all I ever want to do
I would give all that I have to give
Just that night I want to live
To feel your body close to mine
In a lover's passionate entwine
Then I'd let you go again
And vow forever from love, refrain.

J R Griffin

YOU

You are such a lovely lady,
You really and truly are.
You have lots of friends and family,
You are a perfect star.

You bring with you such kindness,
You show this in every way.
You spread your love to everyone,
You give this day by day.

You are famous for your cakes and chips,
You know they go down well.
You never forget a birthday,
You are really and truly swell.

You have a gift with children,
You have such a beautiful smile.
You always have that catching laugh,
This goes to say, you are adored and loved
all the while.

Jackie Ralph

SPARKLY GRANDAD

(For Grandad Henderson)

He died when I was only eight,
my lovely, sparkly grandad,
when he was coming,
I'd wait at the gate
for his sparkling smile
and the Smarties I ate.
He was such a gent,
I miss him of late,
my lovely, sparkly grandad.

J P Henderson-Long

MY MOTHER'S SILENCE, MY FATHER'S STARE

What did I know at nine about the human heart,
to know what I was learning? That my mother's strength
lay in her knowing what should be passed over,
that her silence would survive my father's stare
stalling the anger of the day from flaring,
knowing just what to do with his raised brow.
She was the house with the slant roof under the hill,
and he, the unbent pimento tree
towering over her. Its softer roots no one got to know.

Outside, and in the past, where dreams were not achievable,
in black water-boots and garden clothes, he'd bolt
out through the back door at nights to God knows what,
while we children, ignorant of the word, 'shell-shocked',
braced in the dark, slept off the hours of uncertainty.
Once Mama explained the role the full moon played,
that it swung open a door on his world war days.

On Sundays, after the home-parched hot coffee smell
of good intentions, he wore a different face
to church, taking it off again when he returned.
His best was then obscured by the fear
I wanted to grow up away from and fall in love.
He held the key that kept us from going astray,
she, the lamp left on in the doorway.

Delores Gauntlett

GRANNY'S ROCKING CHAIR

Granny sits in her rocking chair,
A neat and tidy bun in her thinning grey hair
A floral pinny, her slippers too,
Doing some knitting, just for you.
She wants for you to come and call,
It seems you have no time at all

And as she's quietly sitting there,
Rocking away in her old rocking chair,
She reflects on the past of the memories of old,
When her children were young and the stories she told
There were hard times, bad times, happy and sad
She's rocking alone and she misses your dad

She's tired now and she falls to sleep
Her memories are hers alone to keep,
She's a mother, a granny, one of the best
The good Lord has taken her now to rest

The jumper's half knit, there's wool left on the ball,
If only you had the time to call
Please read this poem so carefully
It reflects both you and me, find the time to make that call,
For one day you'll find she's not there at all

Pamela J O'Donnell

REMEMBERING GRANDAD

On the light beech bench
I perch and remember, I remember him
To the organ singing 'Morning Has Broken'
To the first school children running and laughing
To the steady silver river slowly trickling

Smoke from a cottage in the distance
Rises, floats in swirls, then disappears
Just like smoke from his pipe
It floats then disappears

The stone war memorial stands with pride
In all its glory, as the sun
Bounces off the golden plaque
Just like his glasses reflecting the light

Bees and butterflies wander in and out
Of the shade from the old oak tree
It stands strong and sturdy
A member of the village, and friend to all

On the light beech bench
I perch and remember, I remember him
The tall spire high in the sky
Watching the birds soaring free
I kneel at the grave, new every time
And lay down daffodils at his head
Light seeps through the trees
As I remember Grandad

Anya Lees

NAN

From as far back as I can remember
My nan has always been the same
Always a pleasure to visit
She never seemed to complain

She was left alone when Grandad died
And we used to go up and stay
We'd take a look in her scrapbook
At all she did in her early days

When Grandad and she helped the scout band
And all local events that took place
They were well known around our town
And were always friendly faces

Nan's home cooking is what I won't forget
The treacle tarts that she used to make
She always raved about the butcher's shop
To knock them would be a mistake!

She's had her fair share of hard times
But never looked down or glum
She had two evacuees during the war
One of whom became my godmum.

My nan is someone I'll always admire
Her hard-working and friendly life
She was an excellent mum, nan and great-nan
And I'm sure she was an excellent wife.

Vicky Willis

MEMORIES OF MY GRANDPARENTS

I've heard Mom talk about her mom
and dad many a time, and my dad about his,
Alas, I only seem to have one vague memory of sitting on
my nan's knee,
I think I was 2 or perhaps 3,
she made a pretend clock using a box of Dairylea,
the fingers were red and pinned by a kisspin,
I was so comfortable on her knee.
My other grandad died when I was just 4,
I remember his face, a bald head and round specs.
Mom told me he was the best at maths at his work,
and that I have his brains and ways.

My other nan I've only seen old photos of,
she died before I was born,
Dad still cries sometimes when he thinks of his mom.
Her husband, my other grandad, I remember more,
for he was with us longer.

He wore a cap, of tweed, I think it was,
he'd throw it on the floor at times when he visited our house.

Dad had a call from his brother one day,
he was sad and drew the curtains,
for my last grandad had gone.

All my grandparents died when I was young,
and one never lived to see me born.
For years I wished I still had them, even just one,
that I could talk to, share secrets with
and look up to, seeing into their wise old eyes.
I sometimes felt like the odd one out as they'd all passed.

If you still have your grandparents,
so lucky you are. Make the most of them every day,
and every moment with them as they're precious.

Paul Walters

A FRUITLESS OBSESSION

This love is wrong; this love is obsessive;
this love is unrequited.
Or is it?
Each day he stops to glance in my direction.
But is he thinking *Don't go there - she's far too old for you*
or *God, how that woman stares at me!*
It could be either, it might be neither.

Sometimes, as he passes, he says 'Hi!'
and sometimes not.
Sometimes, I go to him with business,
which he deals with in his own shy, sensitive way.
Each morning I wake up thinking
Today he'll be there; today I'll see him;
and my legs go weak and my heart thumps in anticipation of
the sight of his wonderful face.
The fact that he is here, in the same place as me,
seems truly amazing!

But this dream takes no account of his likes and dislikes,
his bad habits or his mood swings,
of which, in reality, I have no knowledge.
In this dream, I feel only his body close to mine
and the passion of his love for me.

This fantasy harms no one, nor is it useless,
(serving merely to relieve the monotony of my day).
It doesn't matter; it has no consequence.
But the reality is: my love for him exists . . .

Joan Dawn

FOR MY WIFE

When I grow old
I want to grow old with you
And over the cornflakes,
The children grown and gone
We will still share memories
Via a knowing smile,
A gentle caress of hands
Of days now distant
When this adventure began
With one tender kiss.

And then over supper,
A glass of red wine or two
We'll sit silently remembering
The photographs on the wall
And you will still smile
Such beautiful youthful smiles.
Then, as each sleep falls
I'll whisper, 'I love you'
For when I grow old
I want to grow old with you.

Colin Taylor

MEMORIES

Darkness spreading through my life,
A widow now, but once a wife,
My broken heart pains me now,
I remember our wedding vow.
How you slipped the ring onto my finger,
Our life ahead, with time to linger,
My heart is broken, I am in pain
Because, I will never see you again.

Sarah Beck (12)

FOR JOSIE AND NORMAN'S
GOLDEN WEDDING ANNIVERSARY

Sloe gin,
Sharp, sweet, strong,
Takes time, cannot be rushed.
Bitter sloes, coaxed to ripeness by summer sun,
Slowly relinquish their sunset blush.

A garden,
Tended through the years,
Responding to the gardener's careful touch,
Taking shape and flourishing,
Asks for little, yields so much.

It takes time too, to weave that
Tapestry which is marriage.
Patient, nimble fingers
Interlacing countless threads.
And through it all
A golden cord
Lighting the dark,
Making more brilliant the
Summer sun above.
This golden filament,
Stronger than steel,
Yet made of that fragile stuff
That we call love.

We have come to know each other so well.
Fifty shared years
Reflected in those
Dear familiar eyes.
And yet, that other miracle -
Love's sweet ambush
Still can take us by surprise.

Jenny Donnison

LOVE

My love here's my hand
Take it, it's mine
Hold it, it's yours
I'll share it with you
As I share my heart
My heart
Take it, it's mine
Hold it, never break it
It's mine
Mine for always
It's yours to hold our love in, our love
Hold it, hold it, hold it in your soul
My love, keep it, it's yours
Treasure it, remember it, it's precious
Never-ending
Always forgiving
Always love, it's ours
Ours forever
Love

Sally Williams

FEELINGS

I mpassioned by the softness of your lovely face,

L ulled by the silvery tone of your voice,
O verwhelmed by the majesty of your feminine grace,
V anquished by your beautiful eyes.
E nchanted by the warmth of your silky lips,

Y ielding to mine in a lingering kiss,
O vercome by feelings nothing could eclipse,
U ntold joy as you answered, 'Yes!'

Tony Reese

MY MOTHER

When I was small you were there every day
Always loving and caring in every way
I felt safe knowing you were there
Your warmth and kindness you would share
Someone to share my troubles with
Birthdays and other occasions you'd give
Always chatting on the phone
Visiting each other's home
By the fireside you'd sit having tea
Watching a film or talking to me
Plenty of happiness and some tears
You kept me safe from harm, I had no fears
My mother, you were a treasure
Always love you forever and ever.

K Brown

CHECKS AND BALANCES

Do you dote upon me?
Like I forever you!
That the fish does the sea
And the water weeds do.
Would you carve a red wood
Into a blind statute face?
Judge, praise, my bad or good
For the sake of love's grace.
The sun naps in the west
But a love, real and strong
Always new, needs no rest.
Though the weather feels wrong
I forgive and forget
For a little while yet.

Kifayah AbdulQuadri

I LOVE YOU

I love you so very much,
The feel of your tender touch.
The smile upon your face,
The way it makes my heart race.

I love that look you give to me,
The one only for me to see.
Your eyes reflect what's in your heart,
When you say we'll never part.

I love you because you're you
Someone who says they're true.
For what I see is what I get,
I want no other, you need never fret.

I love the moments we are together,
When our hands caress, light as a feather,
When lips mould in passion and desire,
That burns inside like a forest fire.

Yes I love you so very much,
The way our hearts tenderly touch.
The promise we hold in gentle love,
A perfect match, like fingers and a glove . . .

Alan J Morgan

MY GRANDPARENTS

Going on trips to the park
Helping with homework and reading books
Watching the fireworks after dark
Crazy golf and feeding the ducks

Offering help, support and advice
Picking me up from school
Playing cards and games with dice
Ice cream and lemonade to keep cool

Winifred and Arthur, this is for you
For memories I'll keep with me
For the late Jean and Harry too
Whose spirits are now free

Christmases I remember well
With each passing year
The joy and happy times to tell
Whenever there is cheer

Your life's experience and knowledge is vast
Though mine has just begun
I'll cherish the future and the past
I'm proud to be your grandson.

Adam Poole

THE MIRACLE OF YOU

An angel fell when our lips first met
She sang joyously around our love
Thunderous trumpets sounded in the background
Or could that have been my heart . . . *thud, thud, thud!*
When I am in your arms I am saved
I am reborn; envied by all who have faith
It was a long journey before I met you
Full of loneliness, disappointment and grief
But now the choirs of Heaven have sung
And I am renewed with belief.
Your strength, knowledge and courage has guided me
Through the intricate paths in my life
Yet it was your sensitivity and devotion to me
That made me proud to be your wife
Our love was crafted with an ingenious tool
As though an inspired carpenter woke up in the night
And created the miracle of you

Danielle Watts

THE NAN ON THE OTHER SIDE

The nan on the other side, looks on in sad surprise.
Never invited in fun or farce,
Just sits on the sidelines and waits to be asked.
She hopes one day they will see her there.
Knowing she loves them, she's made that quite clear.
Her love is no different, her hopes are the same.
The nan on the sidelines never complains.
Fear of rejection, she waits for the time,
When they have all grown,
Have minds of their own.
For the nan who is waiting on the sidelines!

Maureen Wheeler

GRANDPARENTS

Grandma
not only singing *Trust and Obey*
in her clear folk song way
in the front room of the miners' terraced house
with Dad, her son, playing the piano
Mum supporting with trained tone
Grandpa beating rhythm on his chair arm
but her meaning it
that's what I remember.
Faith, simple and profound
thrown to me to catch
as lived.

Grandpa
cultivating his allotment
as well as his garden
silently but with precision
willing and ready
for the novice of a grandson
to help him
accept his unskilled ignorance
knowing being was enough.

Can the Olympic torch
which bore fruit through childhood
burn and blaze again
refining and fuelling
the next generation?

Robert D Shooter

GRANDAD'S SUNDAY TREAT

*(1953 - I was five at the time, my grandfather, James Garnett Spence,
would take me for rides on the Liverpool Overhead Railway)*

'Come on, Son, I know where I'll take you today
On the Dockers Umbrella down the Pierhead way'
Oh, the excitement as we join the electric train of delight
Its wooden seats varnished, all shining and bright
Now begins our magical tour, on to Gladstone, Hornby, The Alex,
Langton and Brocklebank Docks
Past coasters and freighters of every size, and what a surprise
'The Empress of Canada' all burnt out and dead on her side.

So onward we go, on this magical tour
Past Canada, Huskisson, Sandon, Wellington and Bramleymoore
Past warehouses full to the brim
And saddle tank engines in their green livery paint.

So onward, Nelson, Salisbury, Collinwood Docks
Till we reach Clarence Power Station with its huge chimney stacks
Trafalgar, Victoria, Waterloo Docks are next
Over the Edgehill branch line with its Transatlantic specials
Heading for the Princess Dock.

Then our final destination, we reach the Pierhead
Where we step down from the train
Yet, wait just a minute! There's one more treat in store
For back home we must travel on the same magical train tour.

D G Seiglow

A LOVER'S TIME

(Rebecca and James)

The leaves fell along the restful river,
as the autumn light rose in the east.
A look was given which imprinted the heart,
but was deflected by the sorrowful soul.
The snow fell on the frozen forest,
as winter swept in with her icy cloak.
The little light sat silently in solitude,
with a fool's hope in hiding.
The daffodil buds popped up through the lifeless land,
which was revived with the kiss of spring.
The little light then began to flourish,
unaware of the shadow's presence.
Summer brought sunshine,
and the echoes of memories past.
The soul stood still in silent prayer,
as the light glowed into embers.
Autumn came,
and the oceans went to sleep.
The little hope although not seen,
was present still on the edges of the soul.
Many moons passed,
as the little light grew.
Once more a look was given,
a clock ticked; and the soul smiled.

M L Courtney

SCORNED

What were you thinking coming back
filmy-gazed like this, wearing white emptily,
your soul on the outside, just fallen from the sky?
Bored with your cold world you propped against this town,
remember? Expanded the image of yourself:
only surface and no depth. You're skilled at being everywhere.
So beautiful you were, you started snowing.
You scattered your emotions quickly: white lies in your mouth,
fooled everyone into imagining warmth.
From the throat of your words, a season of ice has risen.
You, still beautiful, becoming everyone's dream.
I watched you bend over your trade: soft curves against walls,
your breasts dark on slopes. Melting at your waist
as he touched you, stayed with you a snowfall more.
You felt me hold onto what is passing, and cried.
After that breaking things up was easy for you to do,
the smear my heart left was your dusk.
But what were you thinking coming back,
reminding me how he's followed you,
left me huddled for warmth, and ugly,
whilst you became more beautiful with my wounds?
What were you thinking, winter?

Elena Tincu-Straton

MY GRANDMOTHER JANE

I smile when I recall your dear face,
you were someone special I could never replace.
Always such a great part of my young life,
then such a good friend to me when I became Albert's wife.
So many memories - where do I start?
Each one so precious and locked in my heart.
You were from an era of a bygone age,
today we live in a hectic rat race.
I remember Mondays, washdays when you would sing,
life was hard then - no washers, driers or such things.
The big old-fashioned fireplace where we toasted our bread,
there were two seats on the fender where I sat and read.
A trip to the pictures - just you and me,
Old Mother Riley and George Formby were our cup of tea.
We lived through the war years - I remember the fear,
air raids and sirens, your hands holding me near.
You had a much loved son, Matty, he was killed in the war,
sad you never got to see his grave, France was then too far.
You were an incredible woman with your courage and strength,
taking care of us, you would go to any lengths.
Yes, my beloved grandmother, I was blessed that you were mine
my love for you is locked in my heart for all time.

Elizabeth Hoggett

A LONG WINTER'S NIGHT

The sun's been stolen from my universe
Taken from my soul
The darkness prowls around testing
The parameters of my solar flares
I feel its icy touch sliding over my skin
Ripping into my veins and creeping
Into me

Will it engulf me?
No!
Not again.
The sun has not been drowned
Out, but merely eclipsed

Darkness stokes my pains hoping to get
An express ride to my source
I need to fight its advances
It can't win, not today
Not ever

It's really hard to keep on fighting, but I will not
Be taken under.
I refuse!
Soon, very soon
I will supernova

Christopher David

WALK WITH MEMORIES

He seemed so tall
But I was small
Not yet for school
We would walk for miles
Or so it would seem
Up the woods to collect
Sticks for peas and beans
Picking flowers for Mum on the way home
The time came when I had to go to school
High windows, couldn't see out
I hated this room with no view
I missed the walks and tap of the stick
It was years before I knew
That I was sent to Grandad-sit
As my little legs couldn't walk too fast
Grandad was left in charge
Of Mum's little girl
It only lasted a short while
As he was taken from us
Life cut short from the big 'C'
But if I walk in the woods today
An imaginary figure comes to life
Tap of the walking stick and smell of his pipe.

Teresa R Chester

IT IS MY NATURE TO GIVE

I asked my heart,
'What did you gain
by giving off love?'
It answered back,
'It is my nature
to give. I know
nothing, except to
give. You are not
a lover and you
know what love is.'
I am a lover
and I am lit by the
radiance of love
emanating from the light
of her heart
that revolves around
my soul, as the Earth
that revolves around
the sun to a cosmic beat.

Bhuwan Thapaliya

TO FALL IN LOVE

To fall in love is wonderful,
it makes you feel alive,
You're waiting for the phone to ring -
keep looking at the time.
You suddenly stop eating,
keep going to the loo.
It's such great fun to fall in love,
let's hope they feel the same way too!

Helen Dakin

NINETY-FOUR AND COUNTING

I see the soul inside your heart
The years that you lived through
Two world wars and poverty
When I look at you
Cobbled streets and tramlines
The first Jumbo in the skies
Years enriched by memories
I can see them in your eyes
The endless fashion changes
The first man into space
Such a world of knowledge
When I look at your face
Your body, not so agile now
The once majestic frame is old
Though your heart is warm and kind
I know you feel the cold
The laughter lines are deeper now
The chins, there could be two
Crow's feet frame your deep brown eyes
But when I look at you
Those eyes still have that sparkle
There's always a welcome through your door
Though you may not have the energy
You're still young at ninety-four
I think of all the laughs we've had
With your love I have been blessed
It doesn't matter what you can't do now
Cos Granny, you're the best.

Lesley Ann Ball

MY GRANDMA MARY ANNE

My Grandma Mary Anne,
Always called Granny Davies,
Married Mum's widower dad, Sam,
Soon after Mum's own mother passed,
In 1918's 'Great Flu Epidemic'.
Mary Anne had been set to marry,
Sam's younger brother, Arthur,
Alas, he succumbed to the flu too.
Mother, being the eldest girl,
Had to leave school prematurely,
To look after her younger siblings,
So Mary Anne raised not only
Grandfather Sam's first set of children,
But produced another five of her own.
Mum could never bear to call her 'Mother',
Saying she only had one mum,
Though they were close neighbours,
Gran lived a couple of streets away.
My mother on commencing work,
Relied on Granny for much support.
Taking care of me and my brother,
The hour before our school started.
Played with us snap and other games.
Mary Anne lived in a council house,
So each Sunday after tea, I religiously
Went across for my weekly hot bath.
It beat bathing on our hearth's mat.
I worshipped her at invited mealtimes,
For she made the world's finest chips.

Julia Pegg

HOLD THE DREAM

A cup may shatter,
Our thoughts may scatter,
Across a barren land.
We must reach out to take our neighbour's hand,
For hopes and dreams can still endure,
A binding love will be the cure
To save this place, this Earth,
'Tis our duty from our birth.

Cut through the dross of daily life,
See round the troubles and the strife.
To lighten your load,
Deep in your heart, love you must hold.
Then stretch its boundaries,
And from its lonely prison, your soul it frees.

Take your love and pass it on
And life's despair will be gone.
Sharing love throughout the world,
As new leaves become unfurled;
So too shall this small beginning
Grow vast, never dimming.
Then peace will reign,
All this we have to gain.
So take a hand, let your love unfold,
This dream is yours to forever hold.

Mary Yates

LETTING GO!

I let you go, but you came right back
To take my heart and take me off the beaten track
You hurt me once, I felt the pain
I told myself you wouldn't do it again

You told me things I longed to hear
You healed the wounds with words so sincere
The pain you gave, a thing of the past
My love's returned, I can be happy at last

Things are different now, you see
I took the time out and rebuilt me
You came back changed and restored my glow
But I believe my strength is what did it, you know

Ten years later, I love you more
For giving me the time when you walked out the door
Sometimes when lovers part, you feel it's the end
But take the time to reflect, it may be a godsend.

Rita Hurry

I MISS YOU

I'm huddled in a corner at the prospect
Of not being with you
I need to hold you to help me get through
But you're not here again and all I do is cry
I look above and call to the sky
Maybe the task was too big for one man
Because God knows I don't have a plan
Guess I was fooling myself, I'm ready and prepared
Now, for everything, life is the one thing I despair.

Paul Davies

THE MOTOR CAR

'Nana, why can't you drive the car
Will your legs not reach the floor?
Why can't you come and visit me, Nana
Are you too big to get in the door?
We could go to the beach
We could visit the shops
And take Thomas along with us too
Nana, why can't you come in the car
And not wait for a bus in the queue?'
His perception of life is that everyone drives
They were born with a licence you see
He can't understand why I don't have a car
Mind he really is just only three
But it must be so nice just to go out the door
Put the key in the ignition and go
I'm a fool to myself and I should really learn
But my legs are too short, don't you know
'Well, Nana, I'll buy you a car when I'm big
And drive you around like a queen
We'll go and get Grandad and take him as well
And go to all the places I've been
So Nana, save up and we'll soon buy a car
And I'll teach you to drive when I'm tall
Cos I love you so much and I want you to drive
So it's easy for you just to call.'

Moira Woollett

I CAN REMEMBER

(Dedicated to my grandad, Alojzy Jagus, who died 19th October 2002)

I can remember
When I was small
Going to see Grandad
When Grandma was still alive
And when Uncle Adam and Uncle Pat
Still lived at home

I can remember
My grandad buying me an ice lolly
Wearing the small, red scarf
That I knitted - one end bigger than the other
In his garden, on his allotment
With his dog

I can remember
My grandad's sorrow when Grandma died
His tears and weeping
His different ideas
Like the pressure cooker incident
When living on his own

I can remember
My grandad at church on a Sunday
And then he went to his club
Just two pints, mind
And a bingo ticket -
He usually won

I can remember
The news of when Grandad fell
On his way from the butcher's
Ambulance to hospital
Poor Grandad
Lying in his hospital bed

I can remember
Visiting my grandad
In his hospital bed
His fluffy toy named 'Little Ben'
The confusion
He thought he had apple pie every day

I can remember
My grandad's 80th birthday
In his hospital bed
Unconscious he was,
Breathing through a tube
And the news of his death

Nichola Jagus

BATTLES AND STOLEN MOMENTS

A flirtatious glance,
it's started again,
the heated debate
that always defuses emotions.
Honesty enshrined in fear.
Rejection,
the mantra of rigidity,
of never bending
nor taking that one chance
until fate plays its hand
and you leave us
with nothing but memories
of battles and stolen moments.

J J Turner

My Nan

Little red chair at the fireside,
Winged-backed and rolled-armed,
Where Nanny sits to watch TV, all safe 'n' snug 'n' warm.
The tireless trips to the bingo, she does so much enjoy,
When to us she comes to visit
                    We often laugh until we cry.
We give her treats and pamper her, drink tea by the cup,
Become totally hysterical when she gets her words mixed up.
She likes to do some colouring in a book with felt-tip pens,
When our toys get broken,
                    She'll sit and try to mend.
We play kids' games together, put make-up on her face,
She's everything a nan should be, so kind and full of grace.
The beauty of her autumn years is much to be admired,
Her ability to keep on going even when the day's expired.
She has silver hair, silky skin and a love that shines through her eyes,
A very, very precious nan, and I'm glad that she is mine.

Virginia Aggett

Farewell To Friends

Farewell dear friend from yonder land,
This England though have trod,
Yet though who beset us in speech, or so,
Thy mirth and gestures easily flow,
Let your journey over land and sea,
Be not a burden unto thee,
Thine eyes which fall upon thy native shore,
May not in thought, or mind, which lay before,
Do not let miles which between us lie,
Or doubt thee not, or memories stray,
For that brief moment of encounter stays,
Within our hearts in fondest ways.

V L Rixon

CHILDHOOD BED

Lying in a low, unstable fold-out bed, the frosted lampshade
was a woman's face. Beautiful, cruel; like the Snow Queen;
she sometimes crept into my dreams. I happily traded comfort
to stay close to my beloved grandparents, watching almost secret,
night-time routines. Nan undressing; a Russian doll of severely
rustling undergarments; hooked, fastened in every direction.
Unable even to prevent my pricking nightie riding up annoyingly,
I wriggled uneasily at the restrictions my wayward body might
one day need. Pop came to bed after 'seeing to' the fire.
Stretching across me to wind the clock, he would whisper,
'You asleep, Hin?' The steady, slow turns, always twelve,
echoing richly through the silent house. When I awoke, he was
already up; distant, downstairs noises as the fire was patiently
laid again. I would slide sleepily across Pop's still-warm folds
into the welcoming arms of my unwrapped Nan, who, to me
always smelt of love.

Helen Hudspith

GOODBYE MY FRIEND

*(Dedicated to James, who brought a smile to even the saddest face. Goodbye and God
bless)*

Why were you taken away
On such a terrible day?
Why did your life come to an end
In such an horrific way?
We will never forget you,
The way your smile brought joy every day.
We could never forget you,
Not even till the bitter end
As you were such a good friend.

Natasha Hickson (15)

GRANDPARENTS

A grandad's pride
The church stood high upon a hill, the people gathered there,
A lovely August evening, the weather warm and fair,
It was a very special evening for one large family,
There was to be a christening, not just one but three.

The family had all arrived, some came from far away,
But an old man enjoyed it more than anyone else on that day,
Three little grandchildren to be taken there,
Two little boys and a baby girl to be placed in the Master's care.

He looked upon his granddaughter with a proud glad smile,
Smiling as she accompanied the small boys down the aisle,
The lovely little baby girl who was his pride and joy,
How glad he was she came along and not another boy.

The minister was waiting with a happy smile,
He had a baby also and so knew the joy,
That a dear infant brings whether it is a girl or boy,
But no one ever knew the joy their old grandad felt,
The service and the little ones, he felt his heart would melt.

This year is Grandfather's year and Great Grandfather's too,
But that Sunday will stay with him all his long life through.

Tommy, Jimmy, tiny Chloe, what a precious three,
I find my joy and happiness, I'm blest, you see,
Grandchildren and great grandchildren have been sent to me.

C E Growcott

To Nana

'Hooray! I'm going to Nana's!' Alex shouts with glee,
her little mind is churning with plans that don't include me.
No work to do at Nana's, *her* chores are all done,
there are just hours and hours to be filled with endless fun.
First they decide to bake a cake with flour, milk and water,
two heads are almost touching - my mother and my daughter.
They work so patiently until everything is ready -
they've made a perfect picnic for dolly Amy and for Teddy.
Later when they've eaten, they go off for a walk
they like to sing their favourite songs, but sometimes they just talk.
Their laughter and their singing carries on the breeze,
they pick long grass and use the heads to tickle the unsuspecting trees.
The owner of one voice is old and worldly-wise,
the other is so innocent and sees life with fresh new eyes.
Back home, they're using Nana's bed - I think it is a plane,
no, wait a minute, it's a boat, or it could now be a train!
They don't need expensive props to turn a bedroom into a station
just a few old sheets, some dolls and lots of imagination.
After tea I call to collect her, but she just wants to stay
she wants to keep on playing and prolong her lovely day.
There may be tears and tantrums from the girl who's only four
before I get her coat on and get her out of Nana's door!
They are the best of friends, those two, there's nothing to compare
to the very special bond that Nana and Alex share.

Michelle Shaw

BLIND SUMMIT

the adult injured party
hardly moves the wheel

ghost-gums and a night road
disappear above headlights

through the windscreen
red eyes on luminous sticks
want the worst to happen

peninsula scrub closes behind

overthrown by an uncle
a man who changed the music
cousins not passing the ball

my father crushes the guest
out of his pulsing army fist
and slams his boys back
behind the padded door

his hatred careers forward
to the ancient, twisted gully
on the black side of the hill

at the next hairpin bend
he will put his foot down
lock the wheel with his arm

the prim eggshell bonnet
levels for the summit -
no breath raised in protest

and we lift and hang
allowing death to enter

my brain was one half him
the other half a spectator
waiting for my freedom
beneath the longest fall

my mother supports her wrist
and pours another bottle -
we settle to spill the wine

'Those blind summits,' she says,

my heart was in my mouth -
every time he drove us back

I thought he planned to kill us all.'

Robin Lindsay Wilson

DEAR GRANDPA

A distinguished mentor,
It must be said,
More like a father,
Closer than a friend,

All of my respect,
Placed upon his door,
My dream to be just like him,
My hero forever more,

The king of his family,
He rules with harmony and love,
This man is a legend,
I can't stress that enough,

Thank you dear Grandpa,
For being the mentor of my success,
Our bond can never be broken,
Mere words can never express.

Simon Raymond McCreedy

ISABELLA

Strong and still she stood,
Humpbacked like a dowager should,
Caused by yokes of heavy loads
Borne on long, long roads.

Greying hair in a top knot bun
And a floppy hat to shield the sun.
Lisle stockings, darned and torn,
Flat shoes by trudging worn.

Her face and skin, like parchment haze;
Neck flesh folds as crackled glaze.
Arm muscles strong as razor strops.
Bony hands, blue-veined ropes.

'How was she, when young like me?'
Rebellious and curious to see
The years to come and eager too,
For youth to bloom and fruit to grow.

Now the dusk falls at eventide.
Not long, life's rocky road to ride.
'Come child, and read to me,
Sit here, close by, so I can see.'

Fae Turner

MY GRANDPARENTS AND I

Many special people
have been part of my life
but the strongest bond award goes to:
my grandparents and I . . .

Every week on Sunday
Grandma bakes us scones for tea,
whilst Grandad shares his wine gums
with me sat upon his knee.

Mum's never short of sitters,
Grandma's always at the ready.
Night or day, she's always there,
complete with brand new teddy.

They take me out to theme parks,
and teach me how to rumba!
Their energy astounds me,
it proves age is just a number.

Yes, my grandparents are special
and they mean the world to me
I love everything about them
above all, Grandad's comfy knee!

Carol Biddle

GRANDFATHER

Grandfather lived in a sleepy village
In a cottage on the brow of a hill
He lived opposite the only shop in Coldharbour
A post office

The bus came once a week
Grandad used a walking stick, he would visit us
He wore gaiters, I'm not sure why
Perhaps they improved his status
He had a gold watch on a chain and smoked a pipe
On his head was a trilby, he had a tweed coat
With ink and pen he wrote.

Before he retired he did accounts
He questioned us as he was interested in amounts
How many stars did I get? How much money had I saved?
Did I work hard at school?

Inside his lovely cottage was a huge fireplace
I recall the smell of damp wood burning
Once he showed me his box of medals with ribbons
I wasn't that old but I remember his face
He looked proud but sad.

He used to listen to the radio, he refused to have TV.
Even the shipping forecast interested him.
He had many lazy cats by his chair
I loved my grandfather.

Sheila Cheesman

MY GRANDMA

I have fond memories of the past,
The fleeting childhood, gone by so fast.
Of trips abroad, the sights to see,
Of days at my grandma's, you and me.
Of playing magnets, sand or swing,
Of riding my bike and making a din.

There's no one quite like my grandma,
She is the best to me.
For years she has said to show my poems,
For everyone to see.
Well now I have been published,
My poem, in one big book.
My grandma encourages me more,
And wishes me best of luck.

I'm sure my grandma knows,
That each and every day,
That she is thought of fondly,
And loved in every way.
Though sometimes words alone cannot express,
Just how we feel inside.
So I thank you, Grandma, for being there,
You are my grandma, my friend and my guide.

Love always

Anne-Marie Barrett

DO YOU REMEMBER NAN?

Nan, do you remember when
As a little girl upon your knee
Oh how much love you showered on me?
Hop-picking in the fields of Kent
And on a tractor kindly lent
By Martin, my childhood friend.

The times we shared were loving then
And I'll always remember when
I took you to see the lambs in spring
Your face lit up with the joy of it then.

Herne Bay was our favourite place
Cockling together, full of laughter and joy
The years flew by but I remember it all
Then your joy when I had a beautiful baby boy.

Sadly, as I reflect back in time
You no longer share this life of mine
But as the years come and go
I will always surely know
That you are here as you always were
And that I'll always remember, Nan!

Jacqui Beddow

PRECIOUS FRUIT

Fruit, it grows upon a tree
And when it's ripe, it falls on me
Usually soft, it does not hurt
Reminds me of my Grandma Bert.

For she was soft inside, you see
Strong outside like trunk of tree
Words she said would often offend
It drove some people round the bend.

Don't think she would do you wrong
Just brush them off and stand up strong
I always knew right from the start
That she would always win my heart.

Harriet was too hard to say
For children small so Bert did stay
Bert, her husband, Great Grandpa
He was great, great by far.

The kindest, gentlest, warmest man
I've ever met, or ever can.
To my great grandparents, a warm salute
They really were of precious fruit!

F Ian Tiso

GRANDMA

Do you remember the song, 'Grandad, Grandad, I love you'?
But I'd like to add, I love you too, Grandma.
For I remember the time we had, when we would sit down and play,
and sing a song and go for a long walk and sing as well.
As for a rainy day, with my wellies on, we'd go out walking
holding hands, skipping, splashing one another. Do you remember?
And to hear that sweet voice telling us the story of when

you were young.
And this big hug and kiss on our cheek, and to hear you say
'I love you' with that sweet voice.
Oh, to hear that sweet voice sing and tell a story.
To hear
that sweet
voice
Grandma!

Caz Carty

BARRY
(God bless Hookey Street)

Barry, we will all miss you,
For you were the very best,
You did your fun, for everyone,
Now you can have a rest

Barry, who was Del Boy,
This is how his story ends.
He really was a millionaire,
For, he had so many friends

For if he was with you, just for a while,
He would always try his best, to make you smile,
So Barry, enjoy yourself, just where you are,
For, one day we might see you, swinging on a star.

E B Holcombe

LOWRI'S LORE

My gran is lean and mean and super-fit,
She's regular at the gym in her designer kit.
Legs-bums-and-tums, body balance, yoga classes,
Must help a lot when she's searching for her glasses.

My grandad does the driving, thinks France not far,
Takes *centre ville, la plage,* well within his stride.
Going wrong or getting lost is not within his pride,
That is when he's found *again* the keys to his car.

About some things my gran is really cool
She gardens, sews and X-rays bones, nobody's fool.
But then sometimes she's quaint and really square
Expecting me to *dine* at the table whilst sitting on a chair.

My grandad hates the tele. And lounging on the couch
Knows his 12 times table, 1066, all that, he is no slouch,
Made me a desk, Jack a box and a bookcase for our Ben
But cannot load the video and DVD is well beyond his ken.

My gran is neat and tidy, she irons underwear,
She likes to have things *matching,* favourite colour beige.
Grandad doesn't know about such things, simply doesn't care,
Turns out like a scarecrow, Gran in such a rage.

About one thing my grandad's really strange,
He listens to *old* music not even in the charts,
Winces at my CDs, says it's awful music, hurriedly departs
And has the *cheek* to tell me, when I'm old like him, I'll change!

My friends and I discuss our grannies and the grandad
And how it's been so long and hard, it truly makes us sad,
All work, no life, no fun, we vow to make it easier
By sending off our Xmas lists a wee bit earlier.

Mike Hayes

BITTERSWEET MEMORIES

Once I was young and tongue-tied
I met this lovely girl,
With blue eyes that beguiled me
And soft hair that curled.

We walked together, sometimes,
To the mountains and lanes.
Sadly, I was much too shy,
My heart was full of pain.
So we drifted apart
And went our separate ways.

Even when I passed her house,
From my work, every day,
I looked to see her there.
Alas, I looked in vain,
Until one day, I'll not forget,
I passed her house again:
Broken-hearted I did see
Confetti strewn around,
Then I knew, deep in my heart,
My love was lost, not found.

Terry Daley

MEGAN

I gazed upon her beauty
The radiance on her face,
As excitedly she chattered -
There's no holding down her pace.
By love she is surrounded
It peeps out from every door.
The things she says, the things she does;
And she's not yet even four!
Now her mummy's waiting patiently
To give birth one more time.
Oh Megan with the golden hair,
With a baby you'll be fine:
I can see you take it by the hand
But you'll be leader of that band.
Whether it's bricks or dolls or trains
I know you'll share your fairyland.
Now you've got a baby sister
All I predicted has come true
For Amie is the cutest playmate
That has arrived for you!

Janet Robertson Jones

MISSING YOU

Business trips, I hate them more each year.
I tell myself I have nothing to fear,
But the moment he's gone and I'm all alone
I spend most of my time hovering near the phone.

I decide I'll exercise, do some long walks,
Fill in some time with lectures or talks
At the club. Trouble is I'll be on my own
And it's not much fun to come home to a phone.

Six o'clock comes, no one comes to the door.
No key in the lock, no steps on the floor.
No one shouts, 'I'm starving, what's cooking?' and so,
I just have a sandwich, can't be bothered you know.

The phone doesn't ring and I start to wonder
If he's out on the town, trying to rumba!
Or having too many with their 'one for the road'
And breaking the rules of the Highway Code.

The phone rings. He's bored. Can't wait to come home
I feel better already and decide not to moan
About being lonely, and hugging the phone
And how I hate living on my own.

'Home tomorrow!' you say,
'Take me with you next time!'
Suddenly everything seems just fine.

Kathleen Holmes

SWEET WILLIAM
*(Dedicated to William Johnstone killed in Flanders
during World War I)*

I wish I'd known you
But you were long dead before I saw the light;
So young, dear heart, to journey into dark, eternal night;
Slain in those brutal blood-soaked Flanders' fields
Where bold, red poppies dutifully bloom
And woeful breezes sigh:
'Too soon, too soon.'

I've only ever seen your handsome face
Gaze from a faded photograph, grown worn with time.
But dear, sweet William, some small part of you
Will be forever mine,
For I am the grieving grandchild that you never knew.
Ironic, isn't it?
Whilst you stay frozen in eternal youth,
I'm now much older, dear, than you.

Rosemary Thomson

TOM

Our warmest welcome to the estate.
Replacing our bin when collected late
Watching the houses, collecting the post.
But the things we recall about Tom the most
Were his friendly face and instant smile
Willingness to go that extra mile
Washing his car until it gleamed
His joy at his family and how his face beamed
He'd make time for some words every day
Even if it was out of his way
Such a gentle man to have met
And someone we will never forget.

Vivienne C Wiggins

THE HOUSE THAT JACK BUILT

Jack built a house, then called it a home,
A family of five
No more shall they roam.
Laughter and tears brought it alive,
Then another daughter, whose home it shall be
1936, the year that the chapter begins.

Jack built a house, then called it a home,
A family of six
A lot of years they did sit.
Parties and weddings, they left one by one,
Then the youngest daughter decided to stay
Her husband and babies were the order of the day.

Jack built a house, then called it a home,
A family of nine
Crammed to the brim, then came the 1960s, so they let it all hang out,
Christenings and other celebrations, all came into play.
Then a granddaughter paved the path,
Grandparents and grandchildren went merrily on their way.

Jack built a house, then called it a home,
A family of four
Comfortable did live in the 1980s and '90s held many surprises,
Holidays and great grandchildren, then they were just two
But someone chopped down the beautiful . . . oak tree
So the house was sold on the 16th of October 2003.

Julie Walker-Daniel

GRANDMA - 1870-1950

She danced Victorian ballrooms through.
Her eyes were brown and saucy.

In fancy dress, Britannia,
Carrying her trident,
Auburn hair flowing,
Being near six feet was some advantage.

Red flag in front, fashion bloomers swelling,
She rolled along Marine Parade
On a patent safety bicycle.

In middle age she wore big hats,
Her feather boa floating.
She gripped her green umbrella like Queen Mary:
Everyone was suitably impressed.

Between two wars, her spirit flagged.
Felled by a stroke, imprisoned in a chair,
She became gentle
And managed to communicate with children.

Even when she could not walk
She struggled down to kneel and pray
As every night since childhood.

At the end there were only the eyes,
Big, brown and lively as ever.

I Wainwright-Snatt

ODE TO GEORGINA

(Dedicated with gratitude to Georgina Downs, whose 'Breath of Fresh Air' campaign against crop spraying lack of control regulation has been fought quite heroically in 2003/4. Georgina, herself, is a pesticide sufferer.)

She's taken up the battle flag for cleaner, healthy food,
She's taken on the bodies who were in complacent mood,
And all those politicians who by industry are wooed,
Georgina's marching on.

She's fighting for the safety of our water, air and soil,
She's fighting for the health of those who in the country toil,
She's fighting for the safety of all those whose lives they spoil,
As she goes marching on.

Her energy and courage to take on official might,
Have our support and gratitude for her ongoing fight,
We cheer her to the rafters, for we know that she is right,
And we know that *they* are wrong.

They keep us from our gardens and shut up inside our homes,
Their spraying of the landscape contradicts the 'right to roam',
How can they be surprised how strongly public passions foam,
As we cheer Georgina on?

These substances so widely used are all designed to kill,
When they affect us humans, there is no remedial pill,
And all it needs to stop it is enough official will,
That's why we cheer Georgina on.

We once had to dive for cover when the siren's warning blew,
And the nation still remembers how we felt about 'the few'.
We've been warned of chemical warfare ever since that danger grew,
Now Georgina marches on.

M Reichlin

THAT SMILE (MY GRANNY)

My granny, how you laughed out loud
Head tilted to the side
I laughed so much too, I nearly cried
You cheered me up

Always a smile, always a joke
I'll never forget your lovely face
So caring, yet your pain came and went
Without a trace

I remember all the good times we shared
Nothing being too much trouble
Even when we all played up
You knew we all still cared

I don't really know what made me write
Perhaps I've just gained some insight
But one thing's for sure
You were nearly always right

I loved your singing, so bright and cheery
You always put a smile on my face, that's for sure
Even when we came home covered in mud and banging on the door

I want to be like you
So free, to be me,
Thought of me on your knee
You'll always be with me, can't you see?
I'll never forget how lovely you were to me

Much love always
And God bless you,
My granny

Theresa Carey

HOLDING THE BABY

(For Kate and Finley)

He rests in my arms,
The image of my daughter, Fern.
A small, warm animal,
Little bird
Rooting for worms at a milkless breast.
Grasping air, hair -
Fern untwirls a loose one from his fingers,
Plants a kiss on his apple-rouge cheek.
This cosy creature, squirming
Now, heavy-lidded on my shoulder,
Shifts, sifts towards slumber,
Sucking on thin air and sighing
Fitfully, like a small steam engine.
This
So easy, so natural for me.
Me, who could drop all and
Slip out smugly,
My sleep-trained six year old
In tow,
Leaving nappies, bottles and baby behind
If I cared to . . .
Meanwhile his mother,
My sister,
Sweeps the laminate floor,
Glad to be doing a simple chore
With both arms free -
The first time in three weeks.

C L Matthes

BOY IN A BOX

My brother's in that box, all mangled still,
Like when we found him on the road that night.
The undertakers trudge him down the path.
'Be careful with him, hold that casket tight!'

You were a good mate to me, Barry lad:
You did my homework, played at footer. Swell!
I'll not forget, though pansy flowers fade
Or they forget to tend your grave as well.

Your chariot is smart, with handles too.
A nice crate, kid. Some old pram wheels and we
Could race it down the slope of Castle Hill . . .
If both of us were as we used to be.

Mam said that you would be with Jesus now.
Perhaps you two, on harps, will have a fling.
You'll hate it if you have to sing church hymns,
To make your bed - and all that sort of thing.

In Heaven you can do just what you like,
Skateboard across the ocean and the cloud,
Teach dogs to sing when parents are asleep,
To eat junk food and play your music loud!

They're lowering your box into the ground.
I'm trying to be strong and brave and such.
But, if you're going to a better place,
Then why, like me, do people cry so much?

Fred Jeffery

The House That Jack Built; A Childhood Memory

A strange green train
Rushes through chalk canyons,
Hurtles into black tunnels,
Threads its way through girders
Over the wide expanse of river.

An old enamel hoarding
Waits as ever at our stop:
'This is the house that Jack built;
This is the malt that lay in the house . . .'

Granny, neatly pinafored,
Leads me up the embarrassed garden path
To see the neighbours. I am proudly shown:
'Look how in one year he's greatly grown!'

Grey-haired Grandad,
In waistcoat grey with watch and chain,
Opens a leather case.
'Have you ever seen a five pound note, my boy?'
Never. And never to be forgotten
That huge obsolescent oblong.

In the conservatory, cacti reign;
Boiled cabbage perfumes the kitchen;
On the mantelpiece, a handsome clock
Sedately notes the Roman hours.

Along the main road, loud buses
Surge to destinations
With strange names of secret delight;

In the next-door churchyard, raucous rooks
Strive to disturb the grave repose
Of those below;

On the settee lies a daily,
To whose page of bold cartoons
The eye is drawn.

Now Granny pours the tea
While Grandad munches toast,
Emitting subdued sounds of
Polite indigestion.

Too soon we leave behind
'The cat that caught the rat,
That ate the malt,
That lay in the house . . .'

Colin Cheeseman

GOD'S MIGHTY HAND

Bright, round, immense and hot -
Radiant in the sky above,
Nurturing plants with its heavenly rays -
The great and mighty sun.

Moist, torrent, drizzle, flood -
Flowing from the clouds high above -
Landing shiny, glistening pearls below.
The nourishing, life-giving rain.

Gentle, strong, loud, whispering -
Blowing through the majestic trees -
Shedding autumn's glorious colours to line the Earth.
The meandering, breathtaking wind.

Humble, honest, brave but true -
Awesome, Prince of Peace,
Keeping a loving watch over all of us -
Jesus Christ, our Lord.

Debbie Nobbs

MEMORIES OF LOVE

She was standing with a map in hand
losing her way in the foreign land

The wind blowing her beautiful hair
she looked lovely and so fair

I could not resist approaching her
and said my help was available to her

She shook her head from side to side
what to do next, I had to quickly decide

I shrugged my shoulder and smiled
she put her finger on the map and smiled

I understood she was from Germany
German words I knew, but not many

Luckily I knew the town very well
I too was on holiday, she could possibly tell

With sign language I told her to accompany me
to my surprise she agreed to come with me

Now that I became her guide
I walked with her by my side

I was so happy as Harry
this blonde I could marry

It was love at first sight
to win her, I must get things right

Although language was a barrier
being her guide made me merrier
At the time, nothing mattered
but my dreams were quickly shattered

Approaching her was another man
and into his arms she quickly ran

Now back home, I am dreaming of her
and am still in love with her.

Albert Moses

ALWAYS IN MY THOUGHTS

That overwhelming feeling,
Of sadness and despair,
That feeling of emptiness;
Knowing you are not there.
You fought a valiant fight that night,
You would not let it win,
But the battle came to an end;
To me it was a sin.
Why you? Not now, not yet, never!
So much to say,
Now gone forever.
Knowing I cannot tell you how much I feel,
How much I miss you,
It does not feel real.
Each day, each month, the time goes by,
It feels like yesterday, I still cry.
When does it stop hurting,
That knot inside?
Something left me;
That night you died.

Allison Robinson

HE'S MY DAD YOU KNOW!

He's my dad you know, so give him time,
his funny ways aren't out of line.
So he doesn't fit in like you want him to,
with his toothless grin and second-hand shoes.

He's my dad you know, and your brother too,
but you don't go to see him, like you ought to do.
Never invited, he's just not right, able to cope
if he's out of sight.

He doesn't need much, he won't expect,
not much to offer, but never forgets.
Unable to raise his daughters alone,
them into care and him in a home.

Every so often he comes to tea,
we pick him up about half-past three,
with his 'funny hat' and carrier bag
baccy tin and rolled-up fags.

He's my dad you know, and he can come
for tea, be part of something . . .
. . . my family.

Kerry Barker

I THOUGHT

I thought I wouldn't miss her
But I miss her every day
I miss her when it's raining
And when the sun shines, a certain way

I thought I wouldn't miss her
But this emptiness inside,
I try not, not to show it
But it's difficult to hide

I thought I wouldn't miss her
But a photograph I have,
That reminds me
Of all the things we had

I thought I wouldn't miss her
But those green almond eyes
They really had me spellbound
They had me hypnotised

I thought I wouldn't miss her
But, I look for her each day
To give me that heart-felt smile
She was the only one
Could make me feel that way

B Page

My Mum

Mum
There's no need to feel glum,
You're my perfect chum,
You always seem to smile to the beat of a drum!

It never takes a while,
To get you to smile
You could smile for a mile
So many smiles to make a pile!

Even when you cry,
You've got a twinkle in your eyes,
You say you're alright, but there's no need to lie,
You try to get better, you really try!

This poem concludes,
All your moods,
This is my chum,
My caring *mum.*

Gemma Musgrove (11)

Such Is The Love

Such is the love,
I have for you,
that your loss,
not death,
would make a -
wanderer of me;
and if you,
were betrayal's ally,
I would be lost;
and you would make -
a wanderer of me.

Amanda Kitching

VIGNETTES

Good Advice

'Never stand when you
can sit to do a job'
Gran laughs
brown eyes flashing
dimples in her smile;

baby heavy with sleep
breasts heavy with milk
back aching
in these early weeks,
Gran, paper on her lap;

'Gran, I'm a gran
forty years on'
and as I peel, pick eyes
paper on my lap,
Gran, you are back;

Gran's Reflection

you are my beginning
you, my destiny
coming
you startle me

watching

the greying
of the years
you, my beginning
you, my destiny.

Glenna Welsh

NAN

She was gentle
So kind and sweet
She was so polite
To everyone she'd meet

I used to visit her
Nearly every day
She was quite old-fashioned
It was just her way

Her home-made cooking
Was a dream to eat
Stews, casseroles, pies
Followed by a lovely sweet

Now twenty years on
You're still on my mind
A person like you
So funny and kind

You'll stay in my heart
I'm your number one fan
I'll love you always
My beautiful Nan.

Gillian Barrett

NOTHING

(From your dear captain)

You see your reflection through my tears
You shake your head
My love is wrong, my love is wrong
Your love is dead
I shall forever remain weak
Crawling from my knees
Battered, bruised, and tortured
Continually punished when I breathe
Every waking second
Closer to some heavenly gate
For who knows what, when and why,
Or for where your soul shall wait?
Seeking eternity my only saviour
Drowning in love like a stone
Clutching my heart in your hand as I crumble
You have taken my life and my home
Nothing to show you
Nothing to be
Nothing is what I mean to you
Nothing is what you see.

Claire Valentine

ON MOVING HOME (TOO LATE?)

When youth puts down its early tender roots,
The earth in which they lie exerts no tug.
They lift and move and quickly strike again:
Successfully transplant to other soil.
But aged trees do not transplant so well,
And rarely thrive if forced to readapt.
They anchor to the earth, their gnarléd roots
And life-supporting tendrils burrow deep.
A roughened bark protects their ageing pith.
Their leaves, each year, are borne on ancient boughs
Whose suppleness, so long since disappeared,
Now meets the winds of change with brittle twigs.
Where greenstick youth will bend, dry branches snap.
Secure beneath its coverlet of turf,
Resilience lies vested in that ground
Whose undisturbed tranquillity still yields,
With rhythmic grace, to seasons in their turn.
But let this simple quietude be torn,
(Though not by gales or cataclysmic storm),
By love's endeavour, (sweet, misguided force),
Translating one who cannot live elsewhere,
And now, too late, the aged tree runs dry.
It cannot cope in unfamiliar soil.
Bereft, it withers fondly where it stands,
Content to end its days outwith its home.
Old trees have not the drive, nor time enough,
Nor sap to start again a lusty life.

John Beazley

MY DAD

The greatest man that I ever knew
Died long ago,
And even when the end came
He never did know
How much I really loved him
And wished that I could be
So very much more like him in my personality
And those who knew him,
Always did find
He was a man who was gentle,
Loving and kind.
He had a smile and kind word
For them, every day,
And so much has changed,
Since he passed away.
I wish the clock could be turned back
And that I still could be
The little girl who could go to him
And sit upon his knee.
I'd watch him smile so tenderly
And soothe away my fears,
But I know I cannot have him back
Or my childhood years.
But I see him now through
The ways of my son,
And I know that in a way
Dad has not gone so very far.
He's still there with me, each day.

Caryn Smith

L'AMOUR, TOUJOURS L'AMOUR

So desperate is the thirst
Repeatedly we dive head first
Pour l'amour
Into the world that promises so much
Sometimes we drown, trying to reach, trying to touch
Pour l'amour, toujours l'amour

It doesn't take much to fall for
A discreet smile we can't ignore
Pour l'amour
A tone of voice, an eloquent side glance
And foolishly we want to seize the chance
Pour l'amour, toujours l'amour

The yearnings very hormonal
Become strong almost animal
Pour l'amour
The cardiac volcano we thought extinct
Erupts laying bare our primordial instinct
Pour l'amour, toujours l'amour

We have nights of lusting passion
We live a sensual explosion
Pour l'amour
We throw ourselves wholly out of control
We live a fantasy, body and soul
Pour l'amour, toujours l'amour

The ones we choose often play games
They entice us, revive the flames
De l'amour
They give us a brief taste of vertigo
Then flee having satisfied their ego
Pour l'amour, toujours l'amour

We never learn the way to deal
With all the emotions we feel
Pour l'amour
No matter how painful every lesson
We still let the heart dictate the reason
Pour l'amour, toujours l'amour
Pour l'amour, toujours, l'amour

J C Chandenier

GRANDAD'S FUN

Grandad is such a lovely chap,
Thinks the grandson on his lap,
Not that Grandad says so much,
Just a nod, a wink and such,
He'd taught him to play dominoes,
And other games he now knows,
He helps to light his cigarette,
But not quite understanding yet,
What on earth he's coughing for,
Not knowing he'd been in the war,
Avoiding gas on Somme's war front,
His regiment taking all the brunt.
An outcome that was just forgone,
When caught without his gas mask on,
Now no one seems to give a thought,
For our freedom that he'd fought,
The boy only thinks that Grandad's fun,
And not bothered of the war he'd won,
Grandad is a lovely chap,
Thinks the grandson on his lap.

Mel Price

GIRL IN A BANK QUEUE

It all starts with a connection.
You've been waiting all your life for that one great love
And then you're standing in a queue at the bank
And the girl behind you's humming your favourite song
And you thought you were the only one in the whole world
Who loved 'Drunk Like Me' by the Dogs D'Amour.
You got a connection.

Then you go back and you think about how it all began.
Your life and life in general?
Well, your life started because one sperm out of millions
Made a connection with one egg.
There were a million different possibilities at that moment in time
A million different yous waiting to be born, or not.
But there was that specific connection and now
You're standing in that queue wondering if you should ask the girl out?
And knowing that she's the result of a million different possibilities too.
Then you start to think about life in general
And that's where it starts to get really scary!

Nothingness and then *bang*, billions of particles exploding into
                                        one another.
And in those initial milliseconds, as the universe expands exponentially,
For each billion pairs of these particles one is spared annihilation
Creating the universe we know today.

Then, somehow, life emerges on one planet, our planet
And blossoms; millions of life forms competing, evolving, thriving
                                        or dying
And we come out on top
Lords of all we survey.
So many little connections and chance occurrences required to
bring you to here, standing in this man-made building
Waiting orderly to pass your money over to a stranger
Who'll tell you to have a nice day.

So you start humming 'How Come It Never Rains' by the
Dogs D'Amour
Just to see if you get a reaction
Because, you know, maybe 'Drunk Like Me' was just a fluke?
And you see that look of recognition
And your eyes meet.
Time to stop thinking and just ask her out!

Simon Wright

MOMENTS
(Dedicated to Anastasia Cowper)

Thank you for these best moments
Moments both bitter and sweet
Thank you for those moments
Since the day we agreed to meet

Thank you for those moments
Moments both angry and cared
Thank you for those moments
That we both shared

Thank you for those moments
Moments both apart and intimate
Thank you for those moments
It was clear we were fated

Thank you for those moments
Moments both happy and sad
Thank you for those moments
The best moments I've ever had

Kevin Mahan

GRANDMOTHER

You left before I came home from school
I never saw you again.
My parents split up
sent me to a home.
I never saw them again.

Were you my grandmother or a friend
and did you know me at all?
Your hair coloured white
is all I can see.
In memory I recall.

I hope you always felt proud of me
of this I never will know.
I hope you loved me
and taught me to read,
but no one can tell me so.

Did you die on the fifth day of May?
This date stands out in my mind.
Were you at home
when the ambulance came?
The day I was left behind.

Josephine Duthie

BROTHER KEN

When I close my eyes in sleep time
You will take me by the hand
As in years gone by we will wander
Through the pastures onto the stream
At Turner Beck we will dam up the river
And swim, we will put our faces in the water
To see the red breasted fish, the bullheads
And the minnows
We had many an adventure Ken
In our childhood, many a journey
Fighting side by side battles
Of many an imagined dream
You were my knight in shining armour
Protected me from many a dragon
When I cried, you dried my tears
And said, 'Let's go home Nancy
Mum will take care of that.'
You have left us now Ken
On another journey, leaving us
With many happy memories of you
And you will always live in our hearts
Our thoughts and our tears.

Anne Marshall

GRANDMOTHER

At the age of two, I went to live with Grandmother,
My father was accidentally killed, leaving me, Mum,
And my brother.
Don't remember much about this time,
Living with Grandma suited me fine.
As I grew older, I adored my gran,
My love for her has made me what I am.
Her only fault was her absent mind,
We took advantage of her being kind.
She always comforted our tears,
Looked after us through the years.
Mother remarried and we moved away,
Each time she came to visit, I'd beg her to stay.
Poor Gran, she'd only one tooth in her head,
She made us laugh, the way she sucked her bread.
After we left; her youngest son died of TB,
She looked after his wife and son aged three.
Gran was an angel, she loved all of us,
Around us all she would love to fuss.
I took her flowers on the Easter she died,
So unexpected, I laid in bed and cried.
Now I'm a grandmother, not as worthy as she,
But I have kindness in my heart, that she gave to me.
One day, when in spirit we meet again,
I know my love for her will always be the same.

Olive Young

FOR YOU
(In memory of Nanette Sylvia Neal)

Another year passes
and I still think of you.
I can smile now
although it breaks my heart.
I think of the memories
and the good times we had.

This poem I write in memory of you.
Wishing you were here with me now.
I know you're around
but I need to see your smile.
Instead, I write this poem for you.

Are you proud of the way I've turned out?
Do you look down and smile?
Do you wish you could have stayed longer
just to see us all grow?
There's a piece of you in all of us.
And I know you'll stay in my heart.

Sometimes I can feel you.
I can hear your silly little jokes.
You've left me with so many memories
and taught me all that I know.
That is what I thank you for.

Helen Popple

If I Shut My Eyes

If I shut my eyes, will the loneliness go away?
Will the blackness within let me fulfil my dreams?
A place in the sun, a sun that shines without fail
A place by a pool, with the water so deep and still
A place in your heart, where I long to be whene'er we're apart.

If I shut my eyes, will I fall into a deep sleep?
Will I dream of you in my arms to keep?
Will we walk together to some promised land?
Will you protect me, take me in hand?
Or will I wake on the morrow with this same sorrow?

If I shut my eyes, will my thoughts still flow
Thinking of you with me, with me here and now?
Will my mind rest on your face and see you smile?
Will I watch you walk away, stretch another mile?
Or will you turn to me and stop here for a while?

If I shut my eyes and count to ten
Will you suddenly appear in my life again?
Will a text vibrate or a call ring its tune?
Will your words send shivers down my spine?
Will your voice fill my ears and heart with joy?

If I shut my eyes, will you shut yours too?
Will you think of me and wonder what I do?
Will you pause, put down your pen and think?
Will you take a risk and make that first move?
Will you kiss me, wake me, make me open my eyes?

Anne Rainbow

MY GRANDMA

I shall always remember my grandma,
Because she made so much of me,
I really used to look forward to -
When she invited me round to have tea.

She would prepare a lovely tea,
With sandwiches made with cheese and ham,
Afterwards we would have her home-made scones,
Which we enjoyed with strawberry jam.

She would tell me about when she was a girl,
And how they were only allowed to wear their best clothes
                                    on a Sunday,
Her mother expected her to help with the ironing,
After the washing had been done on a Monday.

Her pet was a lovely black cat called Ben,
Who had been her companion for years,
Sometimes she used to talk about my grandfather who had died,
And her eyes would fill with tears.

Sadly my grandma passed away,
Although she lived to be eighty-three,
I shall always remember those happy afternoons
When she invited me round to have tea.

Ben is living with me now,
I have given him a home, you see,
I don't think he would settle with anyone strange,
And I think this is how my grandma would have liked it to be.

Ena Page

GRANDPARENTS

Fanny and Polly, my grannies were called;
they were soft and gentle and kind.
These are the memories I have of them both
as they come gently back to my mind.

I well remember my grandfathers too,
Ben and Tom were their names;
They lived nearby, so I saw them oft
as we played the usual street games.

Life wasn't easy, the war came along;
we all had those ration books.
Younger men marched away with a song,
while mothers were knitting socks.

When the war was all done, we children grew up;
marriage and mortgage we had.
Our daughters came to make grandparents proud
of my dear old mother and dad.

The years passed by; and my grandparents too.
Our girls all fled the nest
Mary and I became grandparents then
to grandsons; two of the best.

Chris is a soldier, in the world's trouble spots,
Nick is a would-be cop.
Two fine, young men both doing their best,
aggression and crime to stop.

Memories are precious of those we love
and I know from time to time
Chris and Nick will recall their forebears old
as I shall remember mine.

Maurice Whitehouse

GRANNY AND CHLOE (AGED TWO)

I'm a grandparent, two years old she is
we paint and draw
put faces on balloons.
We run to the river, pooh sticks we play
over the bridge we look
who came first?
We make a tent, a sheet from Granny's bed,
hide from Mummy and have tea.
We trampoline even when it's cold
skipping is the latest, 'Yes, she's still only two.'
We watch 'Kipper the Dog' television at three
buns with pink icing, fizzy drink she calls beer.
Her words are still jumbled but we know what she means,
she hates wearing hats
sometimes no clothes at all.
We go to the shops, fairy dress and wings
dressing-up shoes, a real drama queen.
I'm doing my best as I know how
new to grandparenting, mistakes will be made.
I love every minute, we have such fun
we play tractors and farmers
animals from the zoo.
I didn't know my grandmother until it was too late,
didn't get to sleep over
didn't know her face
I want to be called Granny
it's a wonderful world.
Soon it will be school
our days will not be the same
games will be different
but we shall always have our tent.

Alison Hitch

MY GRANDAD

(From Jessica)

Wonderful Grandad
You are so great
You look after me
From eight 'til late

When my mommy and daddy
Are out at work
You give me the love
That I deserve

You run with me, chase me
And cuddle me tight
You teach me the difference
Between wrong and right

You teach me the alphabet
And nursery rhymes too
I really don't know
What I would do without you

Nothing is too much trouble
For your precious little girl
You tell me I am everything
That I am your whole world

So, Grandad, in this poem
I let you know
I love you too
And will always do so.

Ruth Fellows

TO ELSIE

We shared many things together
The countryside, nature
Crafts and paintings.

Now you are gone, I am
Finding more about you.
How much talent you had
The things you did.
How courageous you were
You seem so close to me.

When I paint with the things
You left me
I feel good inside.
You gave me your love and hope.

I look back and wished
I saw you more,
That I did things differently.
I wished I came to you
When you asked for me.
I hurt you, I am sorry.

There is so much I did not know
I guess I never really knew you.
Your poems are lovely.

May your memory live on
With the things you did
That brought joy to others.

Julie Smith

NIGHT WATCH

Days leading to the parting
Were filled with controlled restraint,
Determinedly holding up the barriers
In case all our careful dams were broken.
But dawn pillows gave the lie,
Told of tossing nights of anguish
And tears that were not seen.
We still can talk, can write,
But all are so impersonal;
I need that passing hug,
To watch expressions cross your face,
The twinkle in your eye
Preceding something outrageous!
The days are somewhat easier now,
Eagerly awaiting tenuous communications,
But treacherous darkness widens the distance -
Oh how I long for you then.

Di Bagshawe

SOMEONE SPECIAL
(In memory of our nan xxx)

The laughter that we hear is yours,
The gentle voice goodnight,
Your love has opened many doors
And all you said was right,
Your door was always open
To anyone in need,
Your heart was full of love for us,
There was no room left for greed,
You made us smile when we were sad,
The love you had shone through,
Whenever there's a time that's bad,
We'll smile and think of you.

Vicky Jones

FAREWELL MY FRIEND

To watch as your eyes glaze and fill
The teardrops trickle, fighting with will
Your mouth still smiling, eyes tell the truth
Of the pain, the suffering is absolute.

To feel the emptiness of that last goodbye
Never to see that twinkle in his eye
Not once leaving your side in life nor in death
My father, my friend till my last breath.

A scrapbook of memories deep within my soul
My story to tell a generation scroll
Leaving the cemetery drained, wet and cold
Farewell my friend, my heart of gold.

R S Wayne Hughes

WIDOW'S LAMENT

She flits through the myriad of spent dreams
Of yesteryear's love of frail felt forgetfulness
As the gossamer of lust falters gently
In the sunset of incantations of the soul
At what might have been
In the castle gates of despair, looking inwards
At young couples mingling in the sun
Of faded hope in the zenith of life
Links the angel of mercy in the bosom of probity
To get one through bereavement
Of a young widow's love
As the funeral cortege glistens respect
The pastor pays homage to the piper
At the gates of a new heavenly dawn.

Finnan Boyle

FOND MEMORIES

Fond memories are etched here;
Our names together carved on the bough
Through life our hearts did steer
'What do I want?' is you right now.

Our names together carved on the bough;
Always together is what we thought
'What do I want?' is you right now.
Then, I realised it could not be bought.

Always together is what we thought
Blind, I could not see.
Then I remembered it could not be bought
That life for you was not to be.

Blind, I could not see;
Through life our hearts did steer
That life for you was not to be.
Fond memories are etched here.

Robert Gray Sill

UNTITLED

My Jonny has my heart and I have his
We are far apart, but he still is in my heart.
I hold his photos near, he has mine so he cannot miss,
There never was a better bargain driven to me other than him
My true love hath my heart, and I have his.

His heart in me keeps him and me in one,
My heart in him, his thoughts and senses guide
He loves my heart, for once it was his own,
I cherish him because in me it bides:
My true love hath my heart, and I have his.

Cherie-Katy Davies

To A Special Friend

You were and still are
My Christmas tree star
The icing on my cake
My friend for almost 50 years
But one morning you did not wake.

A kind friend you were to everyone
You met along life's way
Troubles soon were shared
In every way you cared
Bringing joy back to the day.

You had a lively sense of humour
Always seeing the fun in life
You were a super mum and gran
As well as a wonderful wife.

Sadly missed you will be
But parting is not the end
Forever you will live in the hearts
Of your family and special friend.

P A Fazackarley

TLC

Rules and regulations to guide you through your love:
Remember to look below, as well to look above.
Honesty will always insure you.
Relaxing no worry, in what actions you may do.
To be prepared to listen in all areas of stress
And never hand over any more than less
Consideration for your partner, if things go up or down.
Just cause for certain, when you find the need to wear a frown.
Most of all, never be afraid to feel what you show,
Follow these rules then your entwinement will not seclude to go!

Elaine Hind

LOSING THE BRIGHTNESS

Every sorrow knows a heart
broken into tears,
though death divide love
it cannot erase the splendour
of a life spent with you.

Missing you makes a little
death inside my day
and inside my night,
but memories of you outshine
the tears turning to rain outside.

Where is the touch I knew so well?
Where is the light that brightened my life?
Are you flesh and blood still?
Are you photographs or pictures on a wall?
Are the shadows in my heart your gentle touch?

Only the soil holds you close now,
keeping you safe for God's embrace.
The cold, grey stone cannot contain you,
your spirit lifts with the storm,
I can see your footsteps fading on the grass . . .

Peter Maher

IN MY MIND'S EYE, I SEE YOU STILL

(In loving memory of Ivy Susannah Crick)

How I miss you Aunty dear,
Bereft and lost you took me in.
You gave me security, loving care
Once more with family, my own kin.

The journey was hard, now it's come to an end
But how do I begin to comprehend?
No welcoming footsteps softly tread
As mind over matter turns to dread.

I turn, half expecting your wave at the window
The hurt fills my soul, such deep sorrow.
In my mind's eye, I see you still
As day and night dreams come and go at will.

I ring your number one last time
To hear your voice would be sublime . . .
The comforting sweetness non-existent
Unabated tears roll, ever persistent.

My dear friend, sister and mother
You cared for me like no other.

June Coral Dye

REMEMBERING YOU VALERIE

Valerie you will be missed by everyone
But Auntie Veronica, you have to be strong
Just think of Valerie's lovely green eyes
And how funny and cheeky she was sometimes
Veronica think of the heart of gold Valerie had
Try not to think of the unhappy times that made her sad
When you feel lonely, and I know you will, look at her photograph
Just think of something funny, that will be sure to make you laugh
There will be something that will make you cry with laughter
Auntie Veronica in your heart you will always have your daughter
Valerie may have left you sad, with a feeling of emptiness
She would be so upset that you are full of stress
I know she will be in your thoughts from day to day
In your heart she will always stay
Life is strange, it works in funny ways it is true
Remember the times Valerie shared with you
May God love Valerie like you have when she was here
Treasure those memories she gave to you, even though it may
                                                    shed a tear
Valerie will always be remembered for her heart of gold
For she was a wonderful person, but you know that Auntie Veronica
You don't have to be told.

Christine Phillips

WE'LL MEET AGAIN

Here again the 11th November,
Time once more to remember,
Sixty-four years since you went to Heaven,
Recall the last leave we spent together in Devon.

We ran short of cash so I wired my folk,
Dear Mum, no mon, no fun, your son,
The reply we received though, was no joke,
Dear lad, so sad, too bad, your dad.

If only my dad could have foreseen,
He wouldn't really have been so mean,
He regretted his actions many times later,
My much respected and beloved Pater.

You shouted, 'Hoist flag *able* - right,'
Meaning hostile aircraft in sight,
Then that dive bomber's heart-rending scream,
His stick of bombs right across our beam.

I searched for ages in the sea, old mate,
Not accepting that you had met your fate,
Here I am remembering sixty-four years after,
The bad times, the good times, the sorrow, the laughter.

Jack Edwards

EVA - MY MUM-IN-LAW

Eva was a small, chubby lady with bubbly, curly hair,
So happy always to be helpful, for her family she always cared.
Nothing was too much trouble, there was nothing she wouldn't do,
Loyalty was always in her nature, and her loyalty was always for you.
Eva rose very early in the morning, to make breakfast to start the day,
Bacon, eggs, toast and marmalade, keeping busy was always her way.
The house was always warm and cosy, the tea was piping hot,
If there was anything else you ever needed, she would get it like a shot.
Eva was willing to listen to your troubles, to help in any way she could,
I know some people joke about their mum-in-laws, but to me she was
always so good.
I really miss that small, chubby lady with bubbly, curly hair,
I miss the laughter we had together, and the secrets we
sometimes shared.
Sadly, Eva has passed away now, but there's lovely memories
I can recall,
Yes, I miss that special, curly haired lady; Eva, my mum-in-law.

Mary Plumb

FOR JOE

The relentless months go by
Step by wooden step
And yet they fly.
Is it so long, my darling,
That you have gone
And left me all alone?
June became July
And August now.
And still I cry
And turn the calendar pages
And wonder how and why
Life still goes on.

Mary W Vidler

THE WOMAN I AM MISSING

There's something I have to tell you;
Something not easy to say,
But I'm in love with another woman
Who meant so much to me in my past.
Memory fashions her image;
The outlines become clearer each day,
As places and scenes are revived,
And she plays the lead in the cast.
I can't deny the attraction;
Can't deny her compelling appeal,
But she sleeps like some enchanted princess,
Spellbound in a timeless cage.
If only one kiss would release her from slumber,
I would set on her sweet lips, my seal,
And take her in my arms again
Before time can turn its next page.
Betrayed, you aren't, in my failing,
As I become slave to desire.
Betrayed, you are not, in my searching
For that which I long to renew.
There is no guilt attached to me
In kindling the flame of the fire,
For sadly, the one I am missing,
Is the princess that used to be - you!
For somewhere in the passing of time
We've allowed the magic to slip away
And in the emptiness that replaced it
We have little to share today.

Bryan Davies

SHADOWS ON THE HEART

When age had robbed him of mobility,
And daydreams trembled to senility,
The changing seasons became all his days,
As by his window constantly he gazed;
Kaleidoscope of summer's verdant green,
Merged to autumn, into winter's scene;
No trumpets heralded approaching death,
As vap'rous on the air his frosted breath
Hung in frailty, and sight dimmed to
Last obscurity; sweet robin, weep, and
Wait no more, patiently, for crumbs
About his door; though bitter wind may
Moan in winter deep, forever he lies
Wrapped in endless sleep, and soft as
Snowflakes on your breast so red,
Sighs dark December's grief for he
Is dead, and sorrow's icy chill enfolds
My heart, ne'er to be warmed again,
Or love impart.

Dorothy Neil

A NEW LOVE

Show me actions show you like me;
Respectfully, trustfully, open your heart to me.
Show me in actions, how you need me;
Intimately, passionately, give your body to me.
Show me in actions, how you want me;
Honestly, truthfully, make your mind known to me.
Show me in actions, how you love me;
Happily, lovingly, join your soul with me.

Melanie McMahon

HARD TO SAY GOODBYE

I never saw it coming,
The tears that I would cry.
I didn't know I'd struggle,
Just saying goodbye.

The hug that I gave you,
Was far too short, I know.
But for fear of losing composure,
I knew I had to go.

I couldn't believe the emotions,
I wish that I could hide.
I didn't know I had them,
Hidden somewhere deep inside.

My voice was all dried up,
I couldn't speak a word.
My throat was choking me,
My eyesight was all blurred.

As the hours passed,
And I sat upon the plane,
A flashback of our parting,
Sets me off again.

I know it's your choice,
To live so far away.
But son you're always thought of,
Every single day.

Mark Ainslie

YOUR WORDS

Your words fill me and I no longer feel the hunger inside,
they softly lift me up and place me away from fear or harm,
comforting me, till you are almost tangible, standing by my side
whispering words that sweep aside my feelings of alarm.
And my heart tries to capture your comfort in its grasp,
reaches out with hungry hands to take your precious words,
stumbles in its hurry to accumulate and clasp that which
you offer and which is heard . . .

It knows those words are mere fleeting moments in time,
soon to be lost forever in a sea of forgotten dreams
where you and your precious words are no longer mine
and I'm left to drift into the nothingness that remains.
Let there be at least a small vestige of your words
that finds a home inside my heart and rests awhile,
that I may stay to listen to you and you be ever heard,
and thus to feed my soul and fill it with your smile.

Annie Morrice

MARK

You are my life, my love, my whole
My one true destination, my final goal
I breathe you and drink you up
Your aura it surrounds me and overflows my cup
I become you through your hold on me
I want you, my life no longer free
I feel you coursing through my veins
Your thoughts consume my pulsating brain
I give my life to you in every single way
Be forever yours until my dying day
And when my time over, from beyond the grave you'll see
That you were my life, my everything
You meant the world to me

Caroline Noble

MISSING YOU

As autumn days grow shorter and leaves begin to fall,
I miss you more my grandma and tears begin to fall.
You were my greatest friend, the one who knew my heart,
and still two years later, it hurts so much to be apart.

There are many happy memories, I keep them safe inside,
you brought to me such happiness and in my heart you're by my side.
As a little girl you did everything for me, you cared for me and
kept me safe,
there's so much still to tell you, but now for that it's far too late.

There were those who could not understand you,
thought you were difficult at times, but they never really knew you,
at least not the real, the best in you.
Generous and giving, always there to lend a hand, you gave of yourself
for others and asked for nothing, just someone to take your hand.

You said, 'I want for nothing, all I want is here with me,
I have you my dear granddaughter, what more could I need?'

But as the years passed you grew frail and weak, even though your
heart still beat so strong,
you always said, 'Don't let me suffer, don't let me last that long.'
You never wanted to be a burden, to need help, to depend,
you struggled to keep fighting, keep your strong will until the end.

I tried to be there for you, but I lived far away,
but for all you ever gave me, I should have been there every day.
I owe so much to you dear Grandma, you taught me about life,
you gave me inspiration, showed the love you had inside.

Now life without you is incomplete, part of me will never be the same
when I remember all we shared, I feel the old, familiar pain.
No one can replace you, you were unique and life is not the same
I will always miss you and wish I could see that dear face just
once again.

Michelle Karen Jamal

MISSING YOU

I still look for you
I miss you all the time
Listening with attention in the silence
One's small sadness
And sweet joys
In reflection of the
Events of the day and night
To stand up again
Before the wall
Silent loneliness
Closed somewhere
There, in the centre
Of my being
Deaf to words
An insecure nobody
Wanting nothing
Abstract from the world
Perfect and beautiful
In one's hopes
On self annihilation.

Anna Cellmer

SWEET MEMORIES

I lie in bed and think of you,
Wondering what you're now up to.
The promises you made have faded away,
Wishing our love could have been saved, *yes saved!*

I'm lost, so lost without your love,
What went wrong? I ask myself.
Love is so precious to throw it all away,
It's now just a memory which won't go away.

Margaret Lewis

RECOLLECTION

Somehow sitting here in the sun
Brings you close my loved one
Tulips, daffodils and lush green grass
A love affair that will forever last
I look into the bright blue sky
And see the birds as they fly by
Oh how I wish we were like them too
We could fly away, me and you
Do you ever think of me?
Sitting here lonely as can be
Thoughts of you in my head
Remembering all the things you've said
I miss your smile, your happy face
I miss your touch, your fond embrace
I feel secure when you're by my side
Our special love we cannot hide
You bring instant magic to my life
I often long to be your wife
You bring me peace and special love
For that and more I thank God above.

Paula Burke

LOVED AND LOST

To have loved and lost
And been hurt,
Your soul is bared,
Vulnerable as a fly near a web
But the pain, time heals;
The memory lingers on;
Till wholeness comes,
With God's peace.

Jean McPherson

HERE'S A MAN

Once he chattered; merry, quipping
For each morning's new beginning.

Once he murmured; softly, soothing
At each twilight's gentle fading.

Now he's angry, sad and bitter
Shallow in his biting wit.

Now he's cruel, dry and shrivelled
Thoughtless in his callous jibes.

Here's a man whose life is changing
Here's a man whose days are numbing.

She was with him; kind and doting
She was with him; soft and caring.

Then she left.

Patricia Smith

FREE ME

There could never be a mountain
too high to reach for you
Never be an ocean
too wide to wade on through

I would cross the world on horseback
on wings of lead I'd race
as long as I have light to see
the image of your face

But I cannot see the forests
or the golden desert sands
for I dwell in locked seclusion
and the key is in your hand . . .

Alison Mannion

DEAR MATTHEW . . .

No wet towels on the bathroom floor,
Nor your room in a state of disgrace,
Left by my not so perfect angel
With a dirty face.

You made your lively presence felt
To all our family and friends
And the love you gave to all of us
We know will never end.

I'm sad I wasn't with you
On that fateful winter's day,
If only just to hold your hand
As you passed away.

Did you silently cry out for me
To come and comfort you
And tell you that all would be well
As all mothers do?

This question still torments me
Deep inside, just like a tumour.
How I miss your constant teasing
And wicked sense of humour.

I miss the occasional phone call
And the 'Blueys' in-between,
Our discussions on the fortunes
Of favourite football teams.

I miss your voice, your cheeky grin
And those deep, dark eyes of blue,
But I think what I miss most of all
Is a hug from you!

Carol Anne Edwards

PAST LOVE

For many of our months, our hearts beat as one,
We were locked up in love, not wanting to be free.

Our bodies blazed in the fire of our passion,
Our souls alight in the flames of our desire.

Never wanting to be separate or wanting to be apart,
Always wanting to be together, held in each other's arms.

Wishing to spend eternity in a magical embrace,
Wishing to explore the universe inside that single moment.

Gazing into forever whilst enchanted by thine eyes,
Touching forever whilst kissing thine lips.

Seeing a flower bloom when you smile, hearing a child laugh
when you speak,
Seeing my future set in stone before me when looking upon your heart.

Sean Garoghan

SEEING RED

I wish I'd never fell in love again,
The joy I had has now returned as pain.
The ache inside my head is hard to bear,
The love you had for me no longer there.

You found another love you said was right,
I saw her only just the other night.
Her skirt was short, the dress a sparkling red.
Her blonde hair, tight curled, dangled from her head.

Red high-heeled shoes were squashed upon her feet,
Her strident voice was very hard to beat.
To think you said you always liked me plain.
I'll never, never fall in love again.

Christine Hughes

STILL LIFE

Your house huddled under low mauve December dusk.
Negotiating the five ice-glazed steps, cautiously quiet,
Silently twisting the key in the lock,
Stealthy as a thief at midnight.
Invading your personal domain,
Helpless secret-stealer, what other could I do?

A cold dissolution hung in the air;
A dead dust-light on once familiar belongings.
Switched to auto, my lonely hands
Sorted a secret stair cupboard stash: -
Lavender spode and swirling cloisonné.
Your must-speckled books had opened like orchids

But your ghost-gloves lay lifeless,
Bereft of the blunt practical hands.
Devastation looked out on the garden,
Frost-frozen: the crumbling corpse wall,
The raspberry leaves clamped in their little ice shells;
Waiting for their summertime rubies, those jewels of July,

And waiting for you, your deft natural touch.
Silence laid a stilling hand on everyday objects
As I laid your life away in boxes.
I didn't hear your loneliness
When it pushed at the door, insistently.
Seroxat and Liebfraumilch kept you company.

Why didn't you persist?
What triggered the retreat back into yourself?
All through the hushed dusk of December and sleet storms of January
I lay with your loss, under spattering rain;
My winter fragmented, its ice-prism shattered,
My actions mere string-jerkings of the puppet-master Grief.

Charlotte Leather

ETERNITY

I longed to comfort you
While you lay weeping,
At night I'll watch over you,
While you lie sleeping.
Your tears may blind you,
But I am still near,
Never to leave you,
I promise you, dear.
My kiss was the wind
That ruffled your hair,
My smile the rainbow
That fell on the stair,
My laughter the zephyr
That scatters the leaves,
Waltzing towards Heaven
On a fresh autumn breeze.

Sarah MacLennan

MAYBE

Let me dream tonight
of holding your hand
and seeing the love in your eyes.

Let me feel your touch
that I miss so much
and let it not be a surprise.

Let me dream that it's real.
That it's here and it's now
and never will go away.

My dream in the night
let me feel that it's right.
Then maybe it will last all day.

Maureen Thomas

HUMID AND RESTLESS

Humid and restless
Are my nights
Alone in my room
There is no fulfilment
From my days
No completion
Of my thought
No one to kiss
No one to hold
My soul stirs
But my dreams won't come
I am not tired
But I am weary
Humid and restless
Are my nights
When you are not here.

Malcolm Dewhirst

SIMPLY MISSING YOU

Sometimes I cry,
Sometimes I smile,
Sometimes I ache,
(When it's been a while).

Sometimes I yearn,
Sometimes I sing,
Sometimes I think
About the love you bring.

But whatever I be,
Whatever I do
You know, whilst apart,
I am simply missing you.

Amanda Morgan

MY FRIEND

I held you as you bowed your head
in proud gesture of a life well lead.

'Thank you,' passed my trembling lips,
sorry on my heart now sits.

You were a friend loved so tenderly,
to the end.

I watched my tears fall upon your sleeping brow,
words seem so meaningless now.

For twelve long years, you were my companion
now your bed lies abandoned.

The winter of your life ended swifter than I could have known,
now your body lies where seeds are sown.

You are remembered fondly by all,
no man or animal did you ever maul.

You were unique and of you their words will speak.
Every day I knew you, a presence filled the room.

You'll be sorely missed like any human kin
thank you for being part of my life. Now a new chapter will begin.

Wenderlynn J Dawkins

SHEDDING THE OLD, IN WAIT FOR THE NEW

Friends
I'm standing under our tree remembering you
Remembering you precisely as you were,
It was our favourite tree, oak boasting without words its life and vitality
'Nature dies,' you mumbled in a distal, deep tone
'It comes back in the spring,' I smiled in an effort to cheer you up
'The leaves won't return, they're falling . . .'
. . . You turned away to have your thoughts on autumn's cruelty,
without intrusions.
It was here we shared our precious secrets with oak.
Here we had our picnics.
'Do you believe in a life after this one?'
You took my arm in a hard grip,
as if you wanted me to understand you, understand your
innermost feelings.
'Yes, the shell dissolves but not the soul, no beginning or end, we pass
over to a peaceful land of spirits.'
I'm standing here remembering, remembering you precisely as you
were
Falling leaves and tears, *shedding the old, in wait for the new,*
Waiting!
Our loving oak will survive many autumns, many more than we
Love has many faces, shadow of loss, the most beautiful.

Rita Pilbrow-Carlsson

MISSING YOU

(Deceased June 1998 - mother, nan, sister, aunt, mother-in-law, great aunt)

You lay, you watched and waited
It was hours past the dawn
There was no crowd to cheer him
Just a lovely summer's morn
The rustle and sound of footsteps
Firm but gentle came your way
Your heart full of joy was ready to burst
The pain in your body just faded away
You know the reason why I am here
In Heaven you have earned your place
Excessive, the trials in your life have been
But as a true Christian you have borne it with grace
And the blessed Saviour turned His head
His face full of love as He gently said,
'Come to my Kingdom, your place is prepared
The angels await you, your welcome is shared.'

Barbara Tunstall

TO LOVE OR NOT TO

So, this is love then! This seduction of my senses.
Obsessional, destructive, leaving me defenceless.
I am weakened, indecisive, in awe of my emotion.
How can I be certain of the strength of your devotion?
For though you are insistent that my love's reciprocated
The pangs of love I'm suffering, are not alleviated.
For I suffer palpitations, whenever you appear.
And my legs just turn to jelly, yes the reason's all too clear.
I summed it up, when we first met, as physical attraction,
I little realised then that it would drive me to distraction.
Alas I'm in too deep now, can't control my foolish heart.
I am your prisoner of love, held captive from the start.

Mary Goodchild

BILL'S ROSES

I've picked a rose and put it by your picture,
Your face looks back at me again and smiles,
There's nothing left of you but all life's memories.
The years that we both shared, the laughs, the trials.
Those carefree days of youth with all its blessings,
The last sad months when much of it was strife.
My wedding flowers were just a spray of roses,
That day when we were married, man and wife.
We planted many gardens in our lifetime
You loved to see the roses come to bloom.
So now I try to keep just one sweet blossom
Beside your picture in this same old room.
Did you know that when you went on your last journey
I laid a wreath of rosebuds by your side?
I wonder if you know now we are parted,
How proud I am that I was once your bride?

S A Baker

SOME DAY MY LOVE

Some day you will come to me and stay,
all dark clouds cast away.
Each new day an adventure to behold,
forever love to reign.
Heartaches, sorrow replaced with joy,
happiness and elation.
Without you there is no tomorrow.
With you beside me our love bonded forever.
My love for you is an open book, there for all to see.
Please make this a reality, my hope's all achieved.
For you my darling mean all the world to me.
Take this love I offer with a heart true and sincere,
for there is only one of you.

Norman Andrew Downie

Minus The Almighty

Spires that dream of Sunday choirs
hymn-boards sing of concert flyers
chipboard bars the Father's house
this church is quieter than a mouse.

All within is wormed of wonder
threshless echoes confessed of thunder
pews that peer through seated gloom
ordaining only standing room.

Kneeling pads lack priests impressions
pulpit stripped of intercession
congregation ghosts so stale
nursed infirm, so few and frail.

Sacrilege gloats from gargoyle towers
weeds wage war with sinful flowers
crumbling brick gives best to time
rising damp convicts and climbs.

Churchyard camouflaged with grass
a stoical subclass swamped and sparse
their ageing gravestones pay respects
in deadened, illegibly etched neglect.

Stained glass plays a waiting game
- it waits for the name above all names
when cancerous ruin no longer rules
when crowns of paste become as jewels.

Sean Kinsella

Sensory Vacuum

I saw it breaking through a fracture in your mind
Black clouds looming, passions blooming from a seed inside you
Then you went to Swindon.

I sensed desires bubble up towards the surface
Rightly or wrongly, you were longing for a life outside you
Then you went to Swindon.

Absolutely positive
Lost all I held dear
Relatively negative
Now you have disappeared.

I was in my senses then
A compromised condition
Let's carry on until the end
I was in my senses then.

I was a witness to the pleasure that pursued you
Without question, your possessions refused to release you
Then you went to Swindon.

Anticipate nostalgia
Lost all I held dear
Painless as neuralgia,
To watch you disappear

I was in my senses ther.

Ellis Creez

LOST LOVE

Beat . . . beat . . .
Pete . . . Pete . . .
My heart goes beating on
And seemingly shall through all eternity;
Each beat a pain, a rebel cry
Why must I live when sleep in death
Would be such ecstasy?
Oh, let me die!
Beat . . . beat, my heart goes beating on . . .

Tick . . . tock,
Grandfather clock ticks on . . .
A moment seems like a thousand years:
Oh what's the good of season's flight
When there's no friend to share
The glory of it all, or to compare
The golden day, the silver night . . .
Tick . . . tock . . . the clock goes ticking on . . .

Drip . . . drip . . .
The waters still drip on . . .
A drop . . . a stream . . . a mighty, raging sea:
Does constant dripping wear away a stone?
And yet slow sorrow's tears may constant flow
And never warm or heal this heart of mine . . .
Why is it so?
Drip . . . drip . . . the waters still drip on.

Pete . . . Pete . . .
My heart goes crying on . . .
Eternities of yearning in that cry
I sigh, then dare to hope and then despair and sigh
Again. Outstretched my arms to grasp
What's out of reach. Be still my heart
And know that *that* can never be . . .
That's not for me . . .
But still my heart cries on . . .
Pete . . . Pete . . .

Dorothy M Parker

TRACY

Tracy I hurt you so
but if I could turn back time
I would have, long ago.
Things I said, so hurtful to you
I was out of my mind, I hate myself
for what I did and said, I was really bad,
but if you could see my heart
you would see me so sad.

But I am so proud of you, the way
you have got on with your life.
A beautiful mother and a wonderful wife.
Maybe in time you can forgive me,
all I can say is I'm sorry with all my heart,
and I pray we get together soon.
It's too long to be apart,
I love you Tracy.

Mom

Maureen Morris

I STILL LOVE YOU

Why would that change?
No reason, no reason at all.
For what good are words
Without any meaning?
And if there were no terms
For emotions
Then how would we know
Our feelings
Including love?

And even if I stopped
To pause a second or two
Could I change anything
That has happened?
For all I know
I might be wrong
I might not know
How love works at all.

Here now are my final remarks
On this page
I state the obvious.

That which you know is true.

Love is allowing the one
Whose companionship
Has made all these years
Worth every setback
Every calamity
And mistake
Even loyalty and other
Virtues and vices

Still with or without
God's crown,
We would never have known
The depths that lead one
To despair and give up hope.
I start again at the title of this.
I still love you.

Dave St Clair

SUMMER MOMENTS

The rustic gate that parts the fields
still stands until this day
although a little older now
than when we passed its way.

I recall sweet moments of romance
as we both gazed across the bay
swinging on the old rustic gate
and idling our time away.

We knew the excitement of first love
when joy was all we could see . . .
all of my thoughts were only for you,
your heartbeats were only for me.

But now I am left with only a dream
of that old-fashioned rendezvous
recalling the thrill of blossoming love,
sunny moments spent with you.

Joyce Hemsley

MISSING YOU

The winds; they whisper
In the shadows of darkness
Calling out your name

        As I drift off to unconscious sleep
        Your face appears before me

I feel your touch, the softness of your kiss
But you're not there
It's only a dream, a wish, a hope

        I reach out for you only to find
        The mist in the moonlight, the still of night

My eyes close once more
Burning teardrops flow
The salty liquid touches my lips

        For we are apart
        Bittersweet memories, stir my senses

Faith gives me courage to carry on
Knowing we shall soon be together
I wait for you and know the ghost of nightfall
Will soon become my reality.

Marie A Golan

WHY?

My mentor, my inspiration,
You always were,
Someone to look up to,
You were always there,
I valued your opinion,
Always listened to your advice,
You were always so calm,
Confident and nice.

Taken so suddenly from me,
Without any warning at all,
Who will guide me now,
Now you no longer hear my call?
Such a loss, such a shock,
Leaving deep inside such a void,
The tears at last have passed,
And I just feel so annoyed.

Annoyed that you were taken so soon,
When to life you had so much to give,
And I did love you so much,
Why were you not allowed to live?

Anne Williams

MEMORIES

Here I sit, in memory I hold
the scraps, the threads
that will become the quilt of my life,
that will cover me
and enfold me in its comforting warmth.
I see the brightly patterned squares
like pictures, framing people, events,
influencing my thoughts, my actions
and I see and feel amongst these pieces
and patterns my father.
I sense in those soft and gentle
colours reminders of him.
In the remnants which remain
I must complete this covering
of my life
with gratitude to him - a co-creator
of my quilt.

Brenda W Hughes

THE TRAUMA OF DEATH

What are the thoughts
after seventeen years
with the gap unfilled
the missing still missed
the life going on
long after death

but never the same
nor could it be
for death and change
are certain things
so expect change in life
and the same in death.

Godfrey Dodds

ROMANTIC ELEVATION

Elevate myself on the romance
Of this room, the atmosphere,
Heavy red and soft seats,
Jazz sounds and rhythm.
To share all this with you
What a simple thing.

But, we had to stand didn't we?
Your feet were hurting from work.
How ironic that this is reality,
When the scene was like a dream.
This place unfounded

We cannot create romance,
When its spontaneity is desirable.
That you elevate yourself on the thing
Which usually falls below
The ideal.

Michelle Dixon

UNBROKEN

Unbroken
And nowhere in sight
You push me away
As though you don't care
About anything any more
You took my heart
And walked all over it
And thought it would be funny
To see me upset
And full of tears
Because of the guy
You are.

Amanda Jane Prince

THE TIES OF LOVE

Dearest Mother, I only wanted to say
the way you looked when I left you today
on the step of the house that used to be mine.

You gave me that smile, you gave me that kiss,
always giving, never expecting
but then loving and cherishing all you received.

Your first child, taken away too soon
taught you to treasure and value the gifts
of the others who followed and stayed by your side.

You sewed and you knitted, tied family together,
uniting, embracing, sometimes even smothering.
You danced through the days with a rock, steadfast husband,
a sharp, perfect balance for your fragile weave.

Your dance was devotion, giving all to your family
so what now is left to define who you are?
Pictures of grandchildren, distant achievements,
this woman is love, see her wave from afar.

Howard Young

LOVE UNREQUITED

The day I saw this gorgeous guy
He sauntered past and gave me the eye
I could see he really fancied me
But I stayed aloof as I could be
He spoke and asked if he could meet me somewhere
At this I felt I was walking on air
But being a shy and retiring type
I said I would see him the very next night
We met at the 'Swan' and he let me pay
I'm quite independent I've heard people say
It was a perfect day and a wonderful night
At last I had met my 'Mr Right'.
The next date he was late
This can sometimes happen
But no kiss, what was this?
My spirit was dampened.
The last time he left was in rather a hurry
If late, he said, his mother would worry!
Since then I fear, my love has departed
And here I am once again broken-hearted.
Will romance always finish like this?

Doreen Gardner

IT'S OVER

She returns slowly, quietly to the house,
Outwardly things appear to be unchanged,
But it's with trepidation she lets herself in,
Memories come flooding back.
There is an expectant feeling - as she listens
For his firm footstep on the gravel path,
His key in the latch.
But hour on hour, he does not come.

A silence has stolen in,
Tangible, unbidden.
Every room seems to echo her despair.
His favourite chair awaits, close to the fire,
But now the burnt out embers are cold, grey and lifeless,
She wishes he was still here,
But her heart knows he is gone forever -
From this life.

D M Ellis

LOVE

Only for love
In love with God above,
Only love lasts forever.
Love is God,
God is love
Okay?

Jason Daden

DORIS

Please don't cry for me
'Cause I had to go away
Just smile and look at it as though
I've gone on holiday.

The weather here is beautiful
The sun always shines on me
I'm having such a lovely time
Back with my family.

I didn't need any money
All they wanted was my soul
To pass me through the pearly gates
I felt so much at home.

Everybody knows me
And the pain that I've been through
But all that is forgotten now
My body is like new.

I met the man who owns it all
I walk always at His side
He's told me not to worry
About the ones I've left behind.

Tears will turn to laughter
On the day that we all meet
Once again in my Father's Kingdom
The circle will be complete.

Jean Lilian Bramhill

My Little Woo

(In loving memory of my cat Tabitha (Woo) who died July '04, aged 20 years. Also in memory of my parrot Peppy who died June '03, aged 21 years)

My little ray of sunshine, you made my life worthwhile,
My little ray of sunshine, you always made me smile,
You were my little girl, and that you'll always be,
Deep inside my heart, you'll always be with me,
Never will a day go past, that I don't think of you,
Now that you have gone, I don't know what to do,
Now you go free, free just like a bird,
The pain I feel, there is no word,
The comfort I have, is you're free from pain,
Now you be young and happy again,
You can play on the field, where the sun always shines,
Now I know, that you will be fine,
I love you with all my heart,
And it hurts that we're apart,
I watched you die,
Trying not to cry,
I held you in my arms for ages, I didn't want to let you go,
For a change I'm glad, that time went slow,
I got to say I love you, I got to say goodbye,
Before and then after, you went to the sky,
We all love you little Woo,
Glad Peppy was with you,
Give her a kiss and cuddle from me,
Tell her I miss her, but glad you're both free,
I remember your quirky little ways,
I'll try to block the pain, and remember those days,
Goodbye Peppy, goodbye Woo,
I'll love you always, through and through.

Tracy Davison

GUIDING STAR

Please don't go tomorrow,
It's a bitter pill to swallow,
Above the clouds you'll fly,
In the clear morning sky,
Around the world you'll roam,
Until you come back home,
I will never stray,
Even when you're far away,
When we are apart,
You're always in my heart,
You're my guiding star,
No matter where you are,
To hold you I will yearn,
Until the day that you return.

Ian White

LOVEABLE FORGOTTEN MEMORIES

Flickering flames, through glowing embers
caress the mind mischievously,
Wispy smoke drenched in fragrant pine log
aroma lingers constantly.
Snowflakes outside cascade in the icy breath below,
Quilts of sparkling white adorn the land
in an eerie moonlight glow.
My crisp, crunchy footprints impress
the wintry night,
As twinkling light on the distant horizon
meant, a welcome home at last in sight.

B Wharmby

DEAREST BEN . . .

When did I see you last?
What were our last words?
Were you happy, were you mournful?
Was it so long ago?

Though our life was never together,
We were always the best of friends.
Because we didn't have any bitterness or anger,
As some parted couples do.

Thank you that the past few years where
Your children knew the true love
And pride you had in them,
And how you longed for their success.

It makes me sad that you suffered,
These past few years told on you so.
I thank God for your confidence
But why did He take you so soon?

I miss you more than I realise
You went and there was no goodbye.
It was too sudden, too soon and too much to take,
But I believe I will see you again one day.

I'm grateful for the memories I have,
Thank you for the children we made.
You're at peace, I'm sure and
I'll always remember your smiling face.

Miriam Reid

BEREAVED

Could there be, possibly . . .
     within a greater mind
a place, not known to you,
     unknown to me.
     Another paradise
where together we will find
that every past wish and every dream
     will, one day, come to be?
Love was so overwhelming.
     You were my whole being.
     You were all my days, all my nights.
     All my tomorrows.
All my waking, my thinking, my dreaming.
     All my flights of joy.
All - now plunged into sorrows.
Future years were ours, to be
     forever, together, in a certainty,
and every year would be for me.
Thee and me, just we two, not just me.
No reasoning why can ease the pain
     enveloping each and every memory.
No future planning will ever again attain
     that sanctuary of paradisical unity.
Unless, possibly, there could be
     within a greater mind
a place, unknown to me,
     but now known to you,
     of a paradise
where together we will find
that every past wish and every dream
     is realised
and will, one day, come true.

Stan Coombs

I REALLY MISS YOU
(For Lorraine)

Sometimes I feel like
I'm drifting downstream,
No one to shout to for help,
Not a tree or even a
Big rock in sight, on which
I could try and climb.

As the stream becomes wider and deeper,
And it seems I'm drifting faster,
I would suddenly hear your voice
Telling me like you always do,
Sit tight,
Be calm and hold on,
Everything will be alright.

I miss our little chats,
The fun and laughter.
The jokes we shared,
The tears we cried.
Those are moments
I'll always treasure.

Friends we were,
And a friend you'll always remain in my heart.
I miss you so much.

Pauline E Reynolds

MISS YOU

(My friend - AJ)

The musical jangle of the telephone.
A familiar voice chiming laughter
'Shall we 'do' lunch?'

The peal of the doorbell,
Your smile of hello,
Eyes dancing with friendship

The men are working, we aren't,
Time to run away . . .
Relax and chat.

Cadillac air-conditioning on high.
The smell of real leather.
Side streets - you hate the Freeway.

Comfortable over-stuffed restaurant booth,
Big chicken salad,
Coffee.

One very sinful dessert,
Mississippi Mud pie,
Divided on two plates.

My turn to pay.
Hug of goodbye.
See you next week.

So many years ago.
Lonely without you.
Girlfriend, I miss you.

Polly Davies

REUNITED

Spirit
babies

flying
in the sky

alongside
the majesty
of the world

looking
down
upon us

to behold
what
could have been.

Keep
praying
for the living

until

we are united
once again.

Pam Bridgwater

TRUST DEFINITION (MALE VERSION)

T ake your wife's heart, then
R ip it apart
U pset three lives
S ay, sorry dear wife, but
T oo late! Trust destroyed.

Celia Parker

BROKEN HEART

I would not exchange
all of those stars above
no not one of them
for your love

And who can say
what tomorrow may bring
if one of these days
I'll exchange this broken heart
for a wedding ring

If it's written in the stars
our love is meant to be
for your love I'll always wait
if you promise to wait for me

And every day we're apart
I'll keep a place for you
so close to my heart
until I'm close to you again

And I would not exchange
all of those stars above
no not one of them
for your love

And who can say
what tomorrow may bring
if one of these days
I'll exchange this broken heart
for a wedding ring.

K Lake

DADDY

Daddy, can you see me? My mummy says you can.
Daddy can I touch you, can I hold your hand?
Daddy do you like the dresses that I wear?
Daddy is it true, are you really there?

Daddy when I go to sleep, do you tuck me in?
Daddy when it's morning, do you wake me up again?
Daddy when you left me you didn't say goodbye,
Daddy did you know that it made me cry?

Daddy do you hug Mummy, when she's feeling sad?
Daddy do you get angry, when I'm being bad?
Daddy is it nice in Heaven, could you let me know?
Daddy when I grow up, that's where I'd like to go.

Daddy can you sing to me like you used to do?
Daddy can I have a cuddle? I'm really missing you.
Daddy I know you can't and that you will some day,
Daddy when that day comes, everything will be okay.

Elizabeth McNeil

TO YOU MY LOVE I SEND

To you my love I send,
My heart does well approve
The stars where eyes ascend,
To you my love, I send
These tears until all end
Or night can so remove,
To you, my love I send,
My heart does well approve.

Christopher W Wolfe

FROM THE HEART TO THE HEART

(In memory of Joseph Hooton)

I came with all your hopes.
I came to share all my love.
I came, knowing that you have welcomed me,
Your hopes as the world awaited my arrival.
From the day you created me, I was special,
Although I was second in line, you loved me as one's own.
I felt every heartbeat and the love kept me warm.
I heard your thoughts,
I know how much you wanted me,
I know how much you prayed with joy.

I know I was one of a kind.
But all I could do was bring you pain,
A child that was to be full of joy.
You gave birth to me and I heard your joy.
Yet I was not ready for this world.
I gasped my last breath in your arms,
Your tears shared my grief.

It is here I leave my love,
And a gift.

A child so precious.
Hold her in your arms,
For I'm now with you.

Paul Parkin

SHADOWS

She was part of my breath
I went to her in my sorrow
She understood my intricacies
And gave me her soul

I look in the mirror
To find a way to see her
I look in the darkness
To catch a glimpse
To hold her again

Like shadows she flickers
I just can't get a grip
She slips through my fingers
Back into the night
To rest again in my memories
To lay on her own

My partner my dear
Take care in the other world
I will join you again
When my shadow flickers
And our breath again is one

Ricky N Lock

A LOOK SO DIVINE

Where will I find
What I left behind
Framed in a doorway
A look so divine?

She never knew
I'll be gone for a while
I only had
Tears to ferry her smile.

She gave her all
Love, innocence and grace
No words I find
To say to her face.

Far, far, so far am I
I see her, through
The waters of my eye
Her beauty, makes me cry.

Where will I find
What I left behind
Framed in a doorway
A look so divine.

Bradwaj Gobira

SOMEHOW

I missed you all those lonely nights,
Waiting, just waiting for that call.
We used to talk so much - no more,
It seemed we had lost it all.

Time covered our tracks well,
Soon, no sign of who we once were.
Would there be a way back?
Now is the time to confer.

There used to be such power
It fairly flew across the skies.
Every moment was a joy
Filled with passionate sighs.

I missed you then,
I still miss you now . . .
Is the path in view yet?
Will you travel it - somehow?

Christina Andrea

BEFORE I CALLED YOU THOMAS KENT

The autumn day with its sad smile . . .
the swing was lonely in the yard,
and you, my dreamer, for awhile,
you stopped your battle long and hard.

You took a look at days that passed.
There was nothing you could get -
no memory recalled, no warmth,
no place, no face and no regret.

Chances missed and counted time,
and never-ever comfort found.
I saw the tear in your eye,
which slowly fell upon the ground.

Yellow leaves and then the snow,
then spring that we all take for granted . . .
Will you see the flower grow?
This flower that your tear has planted . . .

Eliza Kokanova

MISS YOU

Rain came down heavy
drenched the thirsty earth
the plants swayed gladly
in aroma-filled air
as if you were near
bringing fresh, green
desires for me
to share, the pleasantries
of summer rain.
Wandering eyes searched in vain
tripping raindrops from the green
teardrops falling screen
rain drenched the thirsty earth
but you were nowhere near.

Nayyer Ali Chandella

NOTICE ME

You look at me
My knees turn weak,
But you don't stop to speak.

You hurry by
Don't cast an eye
Or see my reddened cheek.

How can I make you notice me
And be the one you long to see?

What kind of girl do you admire
What qualities do I require
To make your heart beat with desire
And make you notice me.

June Kelsall

STILL

I still want to call round
To see if you're at home
I still get the feeling
That it's you on the phone
I still want to ask Mum
If she's heard how you are
I still picture you in
That battered, rusty car
I still worry that you
Don't wake in time for work
Forgot our father's birthday
Just could not iron that shirt
It's almost five long years now
Since you tragically died
I hope that you can see how much
I miss you still, inside.

Beverly Maiden

MOMENT IN TIME

How in the world could it possibly be,
You had to search out and find only me?
What a task, what a mountain to climb
And yet it took only a moment in time.

You only had to walk into that room
I saw you then, I nearly did swoon,
So tall, so handsome, fair hair, blue eyes
I knew we were on the way to our own paradise.

Those eyes you know, they said it all
They said you are about to fall
Dearly in love with me.
The rest my dear, is history!

Keith Manning

Don't Look Back!

The little white inn by the sea
Those amber lights and low wooden beams
And the rhythm beat of the sea.
The curlews cry, the winking lights of boats
Out there where the stars meet the sea.
The far off sound of a train, its lonely horn
Sounding in the night.

The little white inn by the sea
The clink of glasses and voices low.
Memories there as I pass by, bring a loneliness
To my heart and tears to my eyes.
But I must pass by . . . don't look back!
The fresh sea breezes blow wind in my hair
Wind on my face, in my eyes, on my lips;
Wind on my lips, take away his kiss.

Jennifer M Trodd (nee Abbott)

Innocence

Something taken, not to be returned
something stolen instead of earned,
something precious as love's first kiss
lost in a vortex, everything's amiss.

Everything was lost but now it is found
caught in that moment, a moment with no sound,
the search is over, no more need I look
love has found me, my feet are now on the ground,
love has found me so now I am bound
my true love shall stay, never will he turn the other way.

Memories of my past stay to haunt my days
but now I look to the future with my love by my side
no more need I hide when my innocence died.

Maryanne Paston

TO MY DEAR FRIEND KEVIN: A TRIBUTE

How shall we brook this swift and sudden blow,
    When you are snatched so swiftly from our eyes;
    Nor were we granted time for meet goodbyes:
The Lord said it was time for you to go.
You did not leave our lives with pomp and show;
    Nor should we strive to understand the whys
    And wherefores of those severed earthly ties
With us, who've loved you dear from long ago.
Yet, unassuming, quiet, gentle friend,
    Thoughtful, respectful, generous and good,
    Helping your friends in every way you could,
    You never in your life wrought any ill.
Though sharp your leaving, it is not the end:
    Your spirit stays to light and guide us still.

Mike Fligg

LOVER'S TOUCH

A lover's touch flows like smooth, warm milk
Over a feminine body, covered with silk
A tear appears from behind a closed eye
Beloved so happy which is why she does cry
Their bodies entwined in a vine of compassion
Expressing emotions in respective fashion
Whispers of ecstasy exchanged with a stare
Loving her wholly he caresses her hair
His heart pounds strongly defying death
Giving her reason to draw another breath
Lovers lie sleeping, bound in their embrace
Passing the night 'til the morning lights their face
When again their eyes will meet and hold a stare
Blissful and content because their lover is there

Beverley Morton

COURAGE

Pick up your heart from off the ground,
Sweep up your dignity that's scattered around,
The dream has been shattered, the ideal has gone,
The line has been crossed by too many wrongs.

But that's not how it was when it all began,
Your hopes were high and your heart sang,
Can you recall when it all went sour?
Why the battles began and you relinquished your power?

It's over now, time to move on,
To another life, a different song,
Your value is great, start believing it's true,
Next time attract someone who is worthy of you.

Don't forget all that you've learned,
But prepare yourself for love's return,
For, one day, when the time is right,
You'll meet a true love to share your life.

Sara Church

Morocco Bound Love Haiku

Ouarzazate in June:
Heat haze at the oasis.
Sipping hot mint tea

With sweet dates. How much
For this Moorish mirage?
Throw in a rug? Done.

On our dreamless bed,
The hot stench of Marrakech
Filled our nostrils.

Fez: even now, at
Dawn, branded in my mind's ear -
The muezzin's call.

Countless grains of sand
Mirror pin-pricked, starry, black
Velvet bedspread nights.

Alice Boden

IF I EVER LOVED

Have I ever loved?
That love of woman which is made
Of all things marvellous since the world began,
Of mind that understands the other utterly,
Of passion, tender, yet at times so strong.
Do I know of it?

If I said and it were true,
I have known some women who have thrilled me with their beauty,
And I had given them of my strength and touch,
Had walked with them and talked of things
That only eyes of lovers see,
Would I then know of it?

One day in years to come,
When, having lived together, slept and were so intimate
That she and I had grown to one,
And having shared out sadness, pleasure,
Made the same home, the same life,
Then, by that time,
I could with reason turn to men and say:
I have begun to love.

Paul Gardner

LOVE'S ADVOCATES

How long will I slide?
Will I ever know that her love is mine?
To place my eyes on her heart just once,
See how she feels of this humble man
I attach her to chains which pluck on my soul
The rush of absolution when she's just a little late.

She is the fire that drives me
The life that floods my veins
Will she be the ice that splits me?
Will she leave?

Torment pounces when I look at her beauty
A storm of pain and fear cuts at my stomach
How can she love me as I love her?
I'll always need to know and always fear the answer
I know now that love, true love, never travels alone
Fear, pain, anxiety, jealousy . . . its everlong allies

To place my eyes on her heart just once
See how she feels of this humble man.

R S Parks

JOANNE

*(In loving memory of a little angel
Joanne Savage (Bowes) who sadly
Passed away due to Potter's Syndrome
After living thirty minutes on the 16th March 1985
Also twin foetus)*

As I felt my stomach grow
And my pregnancy soon to show
Feeling sick and swollen hands.
Counting days was so good
To be Mum I soon would
You moved and kicked about
My stomach getting bigger.
I was to be told there were two
Worried, wondering how I'd cope
With some help, I did hope.
Then my blood pressure showed a rise
Hospital to my surprise.
Protein in my water
Scan they did declare
Only one to be shown
Something wrong, I should have known.
Lots of doctors I did see
None of them could help me.
Instead to be told you couldn't survive
Very lucky to be born alive.
They never let me say goodbye
And took you to be baptised.
My stomach empty, my heart in pain
Now in Heaven you remain.
Safe in Jesus' arms, until we meet again.

Susan Ballantyne

So Long

If I leave you suddenly - heaven forbid! -
You know, one moment here, the next am gone
To such and such another place,
And have no time in God's good grace
To curl you in my circling arms once more
And lightly kiss your gentle face,
As when I go from you for just a while;
No time to say a fond farewell,
As I have done a thousand times and more;
And if I go from you so unprepared,
Then here I leave you with these thoughts,
These words, whilst I am with you still.

I would I could have lived a thousand years,
So long as they were spent with you;
An age would seem too short a space -
An age, though long, would be too brief
To contemplate the world we shared.

But, if I leave you suddenly,
And go, who knows? to the 'other side'
At least I'll have eternity, I hope,
To think about each moment of our lives.

Yet, oh, alas, now I bethink me of your ways -
Your smile, the brightness of your eyes,
And all that goes to make up you -
Eternity's not long enough by half
To ponder all our nights and days!

Jay Whittam

SWEET MAN

When you love someone as I love you
There's very little I can do.
I can't move on, I can't sit still
I sometimes even lose the will
To live or laugh, to sleep or wake
I walk alone, until I take
A big, deep breath and make a start
Believing I am in your heart.
Not by your side or in your bed
Not there for you to rest your head.
A choice maybe you'll never make
A way to end all this heartbreak.
So when you're tired of the living lie
Come to me and we will fly
Away, above, up to our cloud
And on return you'll say out loud,
'I love you and I'll prove it too
I'll tell the world that me and you
Are lovers, friends and so much more
That you're the woman I adore.'
Now, keep this close, inside your heart
And know that we will never part
Think ahead, make dreams and plans
Remember I am in your hands.
Don't drop or hurt me, hold on fast
Think of the future, not the past
Until, 'Nite nite, sexy lady' can be said
By you, from the pillow on our bed.

Betty Long

WHICH?

They didn't know which sex he was,
This he could be a she.
He wore trousers and a shirt and tie,
His mother said he was a he.

His actions were effeminate,
His father slapped him, wild and free.
With dress, high heels and flowing wig,
He wished he was a she.

He'd wake at night and be convinced
That he was definitely she.
Put lipstick, bra, eyelashes on -
He'd wish the world could see.

He'd shout and laugh, a raucous sound,
A he sound - not a she.
The razor's edge removed the proof,
She knew she was a she.

The psychiatrist referred him on,
To make this he a she
And after surgery and silicone,
This he became a she.

But now she sits alone and sad,
This she that was a he
And wishes she could meet a man
Not like the he, she used to be!

Joe Hughes

GOD'S CREATION

When God created us
He made us one by one
And after making you
He found His work was still not done
When God created me
He had only you in mind
And set for you a task
To venture out and find
Me, to be your soul mate
He made you strong and honest
So on you I could depend
All through our years together
Right to the very end
He made me the weaker one
Knowing you'd always be there
And giving us lots of love
For only us to share
He took you back one day
And left me here alone
Where sadly I am waiting
For Him to let me too come home
But God is good and left me
With memories so vivid and so sweet
They'll stay inside my head and heart
Until again we meet

Daphne Fryer

FIZZLED OUT

We two are fizzled out people
the expired empty box of fireworks.
The piggy-backed car on its last
journey to the scrap yard.
Fires of passion that had burned
the flames licking our hearts.
Our appetites for love now, but dying embers.
No room for fear in love,
and lust is the haunted corner of your mind,
where ghosts of past failings lay hidden
in cupboards, temptation the key.
You and me the fizzled twosome,
my courting days are over.
Smiles on greeting, love on street corners
melted our hearts and the snows, and
brought out the sunshine when we met
hugged in embrace, we were bonded.
Kisses sweeter than wine
when you were mine.
Cards, letters of love's dying devotion,
dying to be near you, with you, always
now boxed and buried.
To grave's lost love,
hovering between the headstones
weathered by life's love storms.

Berni Crossland

MEMORIES

I am all alone, thinking of when we
first met,
our first glance,
first touch,
first kiss,
and our wonderful warm embrace
that told us we loved each other.
Then one day you were taken from me.
I was sad, lost and lonely.
Then my memories came flooding back
to when we first met,
our first glance, first touch, first kiss
and our wonderful embrace
that said we loved each other.
Then, now, forever.

Mary Spencer

THE PARTING

This is our last day together,
Oh that there were a million more:
Every moment separates us:
Every movement lost to a time we cannot reclaim.
Our laughter is for memory only -
To sustain us through the greyness of reality.
My heart is hollow, an empty cup at
The fountain of grief - waiting.
My body aches with anticipated loneliness,
Already missing the warmth of your nearness.
This day moves too fast - too fast.
Pitiless time: you take us through joy
As if it has never been, through torment
As if it will never end.

Colleen Biggins

MOON THIEF

Who stole the moon from my sky to give to another?
You with your vows of enduring love
whisper-thin,
mockeries of genuine affection
insubstantial as stardust.

Who made the sight of waves a bitter thing to me?
You with your poetry, your rhythmic murmurings
beating on my heart like a tide
your passion a storm in a wine glass
your kisses a tack taken only for conquest
and I a fool for being swept away.
Moon thief mark me well,
I would have walked with you
on the darkest of nights.
The time will come when you travel the shadows alone.

Pam Wardlaw

DISTANT LOVE

I feel like I have flu, but yet I am not ill.
My strength is at an all time low, yet I am physically unchanged.
To breathe is a battle and my mind is not my own
Now I can't even find relief in the sanctuary of my home.
For inside my heart is straining and my mind in disarray,
I've lost the words I need for the things I want to say.
Late into the evening, I have an image of your face,
I need your love so badly but you're in another place.
I've fallen for you majorly, I just don't know what you've done
In my list of life's priorities you're now my number one.
I never rely on anyone, only my mind and my soul
But when you are miles away, it opens up a hole
And I cannot heal this opening, until the day that you return.
For my love for you is stronger than I think you'll ever learn.

Dan Lane

LOVE TAKES TIME

Following me through life, are tears of pain,
Evoking deep emotion, time and again.
From the guilt of broken relationship and dreams cast to one side,
Of love that did not last and fear you cannot hide.
Things I should have done and things I should have said,
Completely confuse the thought process in my head.
Why I do things I know cause upset
When in my heart, I feel such regret,
Perhaps it's because I'm lonely and don't know how to explain,
Or how to express the tears that were cried in vain.
Maybe I just need to find a love that will always last,
So I won't keep trudging through my unhappy past.
Learn to move forward is what I need to do,
But who can I find, to help my heart feel new.
If only I knew the answer I would then find
The fulfilment and peace of a happy heart and mind.

Karen Stephens

THE FUNERAL

The preacher booms, 'Abide With Me, hymn twenty-seven,'
And his eyes lift as if to Heaven.
Embalmed in flowers, her coffin by the altar rests.
In crowded aisles are those who loved her best.
Through stained glass, beams unearthly light;
Lingering shadows and rays of silver bright.

Meanwhile, softly enters he where shadows fall;
Cold and wrought with pain, he bears it all.
Some modern disease, which killed her, he did not know;
Only she was his past love and he had loved her so.
Now, alone he sits, wrapped in sadness and misery;
In resignation of past, present and yet to be:
As the scene reflects in his eyes, his own mortality.

Sharon Ann Valentine

DYING HEART

When some around thwart your love
It's a spear hurled from high above.
A searing thrust; you're severed twain,
Heart still beating, you call their names.
Embers flicker faint for a love that's lost,
And kindred spirits count the cost.
A waning love that leaves just tears,
With heartfelt memories of those good years.
When children's laughter echoed rife,
But now icy glares just cut like a knife.
A knife that does both twists and turns,
Relished they laugh as you do squirm.
Anguished in thought, you puzzle deep,
As guilty feelings disturb your sleep.
'It's not me,' you yell and scream,
But phantasms creep, as nauseous you dream.
Your heart aches for past pleasant times,
When days were just as nursery rhymes.
When soft goodnight kisses ended the day,
You'd say, 'Night sweetheart,' wishing to stay.
Now things are strained, vicious and taut,
Your heart lies bleeding, in a trap, caught!
Where sharp teeth bite, tightening their grip,
With each tortuous emotion, it gnaws and nips.
Each flood of blood makes you wither and ebb,
Barbed tongues cut deep: whatever is said.
Heart on your sleeve, you muster to fight,
Unheard tears fall at the thought and the sight.

Josh Brittain

A FRAGILE STATE

Why him for her? Why she for he?
Of the teeming fish in a heaving sea.
Love's monkey-puzzle mystery -
Since the pulsing birth of history.
The attraction of consonant to vowel,
Two become one then hide away -
Like the face in an Abbot's cowl.

Away on their flight from reality -
To live within each other's heart.
In the bubble of their sanctuary -
Their schemata of dreams and secrets,
Where only they possess the key,
To a place where no one else can be -
Nor ever hear - nor ever see.

Why then did shadows in a cold light yawn -
Casting mischief across that capricious dawn?
Unpicking the stitches of contented years.
Dissolving the bond of their secrets.
Pouring the treacle of apathy, sowing within him fears.
Twisting the bow of her cupid lips in the shape of a grotesque sneer.
Breathing the bombazine black of decay on the golden promise
Of another new day.

Only love can behave this way -
A scissor-handed frenzy cutting strings and ties -
Without offering reasons why?
It's entrance and exit outrageously hidden -
In a whirlwind of truth as destructive as lies.
To begin at the beginning - with love - I presume
Yet, as then, unaffected safe in the womb.

Philip J Mee

APPREHENSION

A lovely lass from loving home
Now swims alone amongst the shoals
Of diverse fish, including sharks.
Although she's smart, I fear her lack
Of knowledge gained in sheltered care
Has left her unaware of smooth
Deluding front a cad adopts
When sights are set on prey he hunts
For pride in skill at chase alone.
I pray to God that she'll survive
With youthful hopes intact as dreams
Remain her guiding lights for world
Where trust and joy and justice reign.

For gentle man who cares, she'll be
A partner prince in children's tale
Aspired to win. For now I see
The circling beasts whose rows of teeth
Are razor sharp behind the smiles
Synthetic through and through while eyes
Survey the scene with evil glints.
She's adult now and free to be
Herself at last, but how I wish
To intervene as though she's still
A child we need to shield from fire.
'Oh Lord protect her from the flames
And let her inner beauty live.'

Henry Disney

YOU ASKED ME

You asked me for my song
and I had no words to string together

You asked me for my dreams
but your smile was my reality

You asked me for my love
and it walked beside your every step

You asked me for my pain
but it faded, when you turned to me

You asked me for my fear
but it fled away, at your first touch

You asked me for my sins
and forgave them all without confession

You asked me for my prayers
but they fell silent, at your calling

You asked me for my song . . .
and my voice faltered, upon your beauty

Steve Gunning

CHERRY TREE

Poets dream
I'm sure they do
Of love under the cherry tree.

Perfect thing
Imagined love
As real as dreaming fantasy.

Yet today
I found my heart
Asleep under that cherry tree.

Seeming dead
In cradled arms
It beat no more, then twice as fast.

Every day
I turn to north
And see that lovely cherry tree.

Blossoming
With beauty's flower
She is my one and only love.

Jesse Raen

SPECKLED DOVE

Creamy-white, your lovely skin,
dark-eyed and direct your gaze
peering out from freckled face,
exudes desire from within.

Slim of line, so elegant.
Lissom, are your limbs and form.
On your lovely head is spread
long dark hair, luxuriant.

Striking sun-spots, dusting o'er
beauteous features do not spoil
but enhance lover's fantasy
their full extent to explore.

Reverse of stars in midnight sky
sparkle in beauty, in one's sight.
Mystery of love's creation
reflecting in admirer's eye.

Dullards, to sleep, may oft-times count
imagined sheep o'er hurdles leap.
I'd number freckles by caress
e'er I your comely form would mount.

Specked dove! Lie in my arms
with your tinted natural grace,
and let me trace those beauty marks
as stepping stones to all your charms.

Jo Allen

FULL CIRCLE

I know that one day
I will be healed
All faith and purpose
Revealed
I know that one day
I will not cry
I'll have given up
The dream that died
I will be whole again
These lips won't call
Your name
These eyes won't see you
When they close against the darkness
My body will not feel
So heartless

One day I'll find someone
To keep me safe and strong
It can't keep going wrong like this
One day I will not wake
To feel so lonely
Lonely when the night draws in on me
One day the things you said
Won't be so hurtful
And things will come full circle.

Louise Hulse

REMINDER

When a small girl cries out to her mother,
Halfway up the frozen food aisle,
My memory quickly slips back thirty years,
To the time that once made my heart smile.

I am there with you, supermarket shopping,
And the tears flow unbidden to my eyes.
What would I give to be able to undo
The past and its thousand goodbyes?

I can feel for a moment the happiness,
And the love, that we all must have shared.
Then the loneliness leaps back to haunt me,
And the lovelessness makes me feel scared.

My life, once so full of your voices,
Is so empty and cold, without care.
I'd give up the world that I own now,
To be back in the past, as we were.

Lorna Lea

THE VOW

It was supreme, a perfect dream,
As I recall it now.
That lovely day, that special way
We made our solemn vow.

You had my heart, right from the start,
All those years ago.
It was so dear, it was so clear,
We loved each other so.

I promised you that I'd be true
And only death would sever,
Yet though I'm left, alone, bereft,
My love goes on forever.

My heart is cold with none to hold,
As I held you before,
Each night I miss your tender kiss
And love you even more.

Frank Jensen

NEARNESS OF YOU

The warmth of your body, when you are sleeping
Carries to me the scent of your skin.
Silver by moonlight, half hidden in darkness,
My fingers trace patterns, gliding like skaters.

Rhythmic in the quietness, the sound of your breathing
Rising and falling with the barest of movement.
Stirring in sleep, some half remembered dreaming,
My lips brush your skin, the gentlest of touches.

Inhaling your sweetness, the warm musky odour
With lingering traces of daytime encounters.
Lunchtime appointments, crowded trains and perfume,
Chasing round in my mind, those endless possibilities.

I know I could wake you with no recriminations,
Your body would join mine in sleepy embracing.
Rhythmic in the quietness, the sound of our loving,
But knowing's enough, and I leave you there, lying.

Siaran Leigh

WHAT IS LOVE?

Love is stealthy, love is wise,
It comes in any shape or guise,
Love is mighty, love is weak,
It ensnares both strong and meek.

Love is artful, love is fun,
It can glitter like the sun.
Love is gentle, love is hard,
It strikes when you are off your guard.

Love is wary, love is strong,
It can kill or drive you along.
Love is cruel, love is bright,
It can blind or broaden your sight.

Love is idle, love is quick,
It can make you well or sick.
But love is beautiful and love is rare,
And, for the fortunate, is ever there.

S J Dodwell

TIMELESS END

She went away
To another life,
Another time,
Where memory crystallises,
And personal antenna
Attempts bewildering messages
Of heartaches, desires,
And yesterday's thoughts.
Spirit-free, yet confined
By an invisible barrier.

Whilst he, grief-stricken,
Disturbed, angry;
With guilt,
Born of occasional complacency,
Dragging forever
At his tormented conscience,
Beseeches the gods of irony
And permanence;
For he can only visit her
In his dreams.

Raymond W Seaton

CLOUDS HAVE PASSED BY

Clouds have passed by,
Your tears I cry.
Cloud dark above,
You were the one I loved,
Please come back to me,
You are my true love.

The days are slow,
My heart's in pain,
My tears I weep,
Come down like rain.

The days pass by,
You were my joy,
You were all I lived for.
But now, you've gone,
Lonely days from now on.
I loved you so much,
You were the one.

M Woolvin

Moments Of Love

When we experience moments of love:
considering that love does not grow on trees.
Do we really appreciate that moment, or
is it, for us, just a flash of a passing moment,
to lie dormant in the mind, or perhaps
be captured by the unconscious mind, used
at a later date to entice real moments
of love, pleasure and happiness.
Do we make use of our experience of
love and pleasure, or do we leave
unfulfilled on long, beautiful, summer evenings,
the hours which seemed to us that there
might be a hint of love and pleasure.
Yet, such beautiful hours are not, by
a long chalk, wasted. When new moments of
love present themselves which would ordinarily
pass by, leaving the base for a solid consistency
of a rich orchestration, prolonging themselves
into classic examples of love which we
capture now and again, through our unconscious
mind. This love continues to exist and is
sent via that stream from the unconscious
into the conscious mind, becoming great
moments of love and pleasure.

Gerard Kenny

DISTANT SUMMER

A day well spent
The clouds had moved away
Over a restless sea
My destination a small cove
Carved out of a chalk cliff
A quiet place of repose
Nevertheless, it was summer
He called me then
He was calling me now.
He called me whispering of autumn
The cooler winds replacing
The soft breezes of summer
Eternity was on our brows
Our eyes tender with love and true
He said, 'I will always come back to you.'
He left for far-off lands.
And lying on the tender soft sands
With a rising tide, my arms flung wide
To embrace the spring.
Thunder of war became my pain
Until I could see him again.
Flight-Lieutenant airforce blue
A Spitfire claimed him, a missing plane
How could I survive life again?
The heavens above
Sent this message of love
He's always there, I feel him close
As when we shared those other days
For life goes on and the memory stays.

Joan Hands

I LOVE YOU MORE THAN WORDS CAN SAY . . .

An iridescent light touches
gentle waters
a cascade of ripples
rush and wave to the shore
then dissolve . . .
the light dances
in unique formation
never to return
the same light again
this perfect dance
to a soundless tune
ancient steps
one body
one song
sung in silence

I love you more than words can say . . .

Helen Joanne Lynn Thorn

MISSING YOU

This place never changes, it's always the same.
So tranquil and peaceful, I return yet again.
Memories unfold as I stare out to sea,
No longer us, now it's just me.
Not for the first time I ask myself why,
We never had chance to say goodbye.

Susie Field

LOVE - FUNNY LOVE

Yesterday I was a king
In a kingdom of riches
The world was at my feet
The sky was full of beauty
Poetry, songs and music
Were in my heart
To live in a garden of delight.
            - I was in love -
Today I am a beggar
In a desolate winter lane
Crying in despair
To console my pain.
                Tomorrow will come
And only fate will tell
If I will stay in a winter lane
Or be a king again.

Steve Emanuel

UNTITLED

Precious are the memories of a loved one gone to rest
Every single one being simply the best
Remember when . . . ah that was fun
What a laugh for everyone
No longer here, our lives to share
But yet not far . . . just over there
Yes, precious are the memories

Isobel Hunter

THE HUNTER

I see you across the room, you have a certain air.
I try to catch your eye, but you seem to miss my stare.

I want to talk to you, ask you your name,
Where you have come from and if I can see you again.

I decide tonight I'll make my move and step out onto the floor,
But as I do doubts ensue, and I retreat again once more.

Every week for me it's the same, I am the hunter and you are my game.
But you are unlike my other prey; you're always the one that got away.

Not tonight, you shall be mine; for if you were not it would be a crime.
As I approach you softly stare, of my presence you are all too aware.

I open my mouth to say a witty line, but as I invite them out
my words they decline.
I stand there awkward and want to retreat, then a voice inside shouts,
'Do it, let's not be beat!'

I say hello in a pitiful mutter, I confuse my words and nervously stutter.
You just smile and take control, your aura consumes me, it swallows
me whole.

As we chat, your soft words reassure. I read your body language
it's telling me more.
Am I in love? This feels so right! But how can it be?
I've know you less than a night!

I really don't know but can't resist your draw.
It is as if you hold the key to my heart, and have flung open the door.

Robbie Shorey

SEEKING BEAUTY

As a child that springs forth in my mother's womb,
Born with simple perfection like all of us
As a child I grew up with my family
From whence my virtues spring forth
As a child of simple understanding, as my family thought
I learned simple affection and love
As a child as a boy who understands simple affection
And love; that cometh from family
I gave my peers kindness, generosity, love and understanding
From whence springs forth in my family and school
As a boy who grew up to be a young man, with my family
And peers; from whence my understanding of universal love,
Courage and understandings spring forth
And I learned to appreciate beauty without malice
As a young man meant to be a grown-up man
And as a learned man of God.
I learned to seek beauty as my companion
I courted beauty with respect for I am a man of God
I smiled at her and speak to her with humility,
Understanding and universal love that spring forth
In my family, my peers, my school and my knowledge of God
As a man courting beauty, I was astonished and amazed
To see beauty in beauty
For my family, my peers, my school and my god teaches me
To see beauty. and seek beauty in all of creation
And that beauty might appreciate my offer
Of simple love, understanding and of security
From whence spring forth in my family, my peers, my school
And of God.

Machiavelli G Dayuupay

LOVE LOST . . .

How you tell me the words that I need to hear,
please let them stop, before the pain draws too near.
Because as I listen to you now and then say goodbye,
it makes my heart feel full, full of tears to cry.

For hurried phone calls are all that I have of you,
how bittersweet the pain, how it leaves me so blue.
If the calls would only stop, then how happy I'd be,
no more painful tears, for my heart would be free.

You made your choice all those years ago,
but lo' your heart still pines for me so.
To know I'm unhappy, to know I'm feeling down,
does it bring you sorrow, does your smile cover a frown.

So is our friendship a notion that I must forget?
As your infinite 'I love you's' still fill me with regret.
Because so many other people and broken hearts that you've sown,
your strong feelings for me, never etched in stone.

Please forgive me my words, as they spill on this page,
these feelings released, though still caught by your cage.
I hope our friendship will stand through the long test of time,
but though you may have my heart, I'll never let you be mine.

Jonathan Lobo

TRUE LOVE

What magic spell have you cast over me?
Each graceful movement of your supple frame,
a ballet dancer's classic fluid grace,
etched indelibly in entranced mind's screen:
your mystic power holds me on thraldom's leash.
Like a fly ensnared in vicious spider's web
I agitate to break free of this vice,
but get enmeshed, entangled more and more
in steely silk strands of my love for you;
knowing full well your heart's not mine to dwell
but someone else reigns there supreme to sway,
my heart - rebellious horse - breaks from my head;
a dragonfly rushing towards the flame
of unrequited love to seek its doom;
a stag parched after long chase, hopelessly
darts after distant mirage - water false;
hoping against all hopes for change of heart
each aching moment spent in naïve belief.

But I would rather not be rid of this
emotion intense, bitter-sweet heart's vibes;
a poison nectarine of one-way love
wishing her well wherever she is placed.
True love that soars above yearning of self.

Nithie Victor

NOW WE ARE ONE

No longer together, but never apart
You'll always be with me, here in my heart.
Memories of us will revive.
They're more than enough to keep us alive.

You were my life, my lover, my friend,
My hope and my strength will never end,
Without you there's nothing, a black empty void.
Not making a sound, not making a noise.

I'm so sorry I've gone but I'm always around.
I'm the mark that you make, when your feet touch the ground.
In the breaths that you take from the cries that you make,
In the nights you don't sleep, when you're lying awake.

Please remember the times when our hearts were entwined,
Lovers and friends, our love so defined.
No future, just past; the present will last.
Moments so precious, forever will pass.

The look in our eyes could never disguise,
The thoughts we were feeling. The tears that we cried,
For times never known, we're left on our own.
The future has gone, we're both so alone.

And now we are one, but I know there are two,
In all that you say and see and you do.
Take strength from us and build on tomorrow,
Always remembering the feelings of sorrow.

Paul Curnin

PANDORA'S BOX

Innate sadness in the picking up
And simply handling photographs,
To look at me and you and ours
Between the years of monochrome
Then colour into the morose.
Why dids, if onlys, maybes.
Family life yet ours extreme
Children gone though never gone;
He is doing well despite, and
Darling grandsons on the telephone
Above frenetic lives cried out.
Life now in older ebb of years
Out of synch with early plans
Illness mine, but borne by you,
I never thought that life . . .
Which all seems so unfair.
Pathways lost, refound, amidst
The world's chaotic unending grief
Shares in which we own aplenty,
Brightest times despite the clouds.
I've seen enough, I'm tired now
Close Pandora up once more
For ours is a life to live, with
Comfort in shared love and oneness
Defying the longest odds and frailty
Amongst wheelchair, stick and tears.

Graham J Bedford

IN MY HEART YOU WILL ALWAYS BE

(Dedicated to my wife Julie)

When I am alone, by myself
In a crowd or at a PC
Down the street, or up a tree
Eating food or watching TV
In the bath, working at my desk
In my heart you will always be.

I'm upstairs, you're downstairs
I'm doing this, you're doing that
I love this, you love that
So much time apart
But never closer in spirit
In my heart you will always be

Knowing you're there
Knowing I'm here
Just a call away
Just down the hallway
As long as you're there
In my heart you will always be

We share so much
A smile here, a tear there
Pain and suffering
Love and laughter
Everything and more
In my heart you will always be

What I'm trying to say
Wherever you are
Whatever you do
Wherever I am
Whatever I do
In my heart you will always be

Dave Maguire

SATURDAY LOVE

All the week
I had looked forward
to Saturday,
hoping you'd accept
my invitation.

All the week
I had been so busy
for Saturday,
making plans for
a wonderful day out.

All the week
I had been dreaming
of Saturday,
thrilled you might be
my companion.

All the week
I had been living
just for Saturday;
then you said
you couldn't come!

Alone then, that week
I didn't go out
on Saturday -
although the love
was still there,
I hadn't the heart left
to go.

Edward Fursdon

WORDS ON A PIECE OF PAPER

Words on a piece of paper
separately meaningless, not making sense,
jumbling together in their defence,
just words on a piece of paper.

Words on a piece of paper
saying that you're leaving
me bereft, grieving.
No elucidation,
reason, explanation,
just words on a piece of paper.

Tears on a piece of paper,
dropping, spotting,
never stopping,
empty, void,
distraught, destroyed
by words on a piece of paper.

Kay Seeley

POETIC WEDDING SPEECH

This wedding
Is the happiest day of my life;
To see this lovely lady
Become my wife,
Is the best thing I've ever done,
Ending with a lovely honeymoon
Under the sun.

She has a lovely personality;
That's what attracted me to her in the first place.
She has a lovely face,
Consisting of beautiful eyes, nose and lips,
And she has an enchanting kiss,
Which blew me away.
That is why, on this special day,
I've come to marry you,
And say those special words:
I do.

Jason Pointing

FALLING

He fell out of love
and is still falling.
She pushed him
and wished she hadn't.
He hates her
for making him unable to stay.
She hates herself
for letting him leave.
He would like to go back
but knows he never can.
She would do anything to get him back
but doesn't know how.
She still feels he is the *'one'*
while he has convinced himself
the *'one'* doesn't exist.
So they are both left
travelling the path
where innocents are used as substitutes
until the game ends.

Ian Benjamin

INFORMATION

We hope you have enjoyed reading this book - and that you will continue to enjoy it in the coming years.

If you like reading and writing poetry drop us a line, or give us a call, and we'll send you a free information pack.

Alternatively if you would like to order further copies of this book or any of our other titles, then please give us a call or log onto our website at www.forwardpress.co.uk

Anchor Books Information
Remus House
Coltsfoot Drive
Peterborough
PE2 9JX
(01733) 898102